D1312670

America the Beautiful
In the Words of
Robert F. Kennedy

America the Beautiful

In the Words of
Robert F. Kennedy

Published by G. P. Putnam's Sons, New York
In association with Country Beautiful Foundation, Inc., Waukesha, Wisconsin

917.303
Kennedy

COUNTRY BEAUTIFUL: *Publisher and Editorial Director*: Michael P. Dineen; *Executive Editor*: Robert L. Polley; *Senior Editors*: Kenneth L. Schmitz, James H. Robb; *Associate Editor*: Dorothy Hennessy; *Editorial Assistant*: Carolyn Johnson; *Director of Sales*: John Dineen; *Circulation Manager*: Trudy Schnittka; *Fulfillment*: Marlene Yogerst; *Editorial Secretary*: Donna Johnson.

The Editors are grateful to the following publishers for permission to include the following copyright material in this volume: Doubleday and Company, Inc., for excerpts from *To Seek a Newer World* by Robert F. Kennedy. Copyright © 1967 by Robert F. Kennedy. Reprinted by permission of Doubleday and Company, Inc. *Saturday Review* for excerpt from "A Free Trade in Ideas" by Robert F. Kennedy. Copyright 1963 by *Saturday Review*, Inc.

PHOTO CREDITS

All photos by Black Star Publishing Company, Incorporated, with the exception of the following: State of Alabama, 75 (bottom); Richard Hall, 17; M. Hammes, 27; Algimantas Kezys, S. J., 25, 37, 42, 56, 58, 62, 76 (bottom); Hans Knopf, PIX Incorporated, 19; Martin Marietta Corporation, 26; *The Milwaukee Journal*, 47, 75 (top); 77; David Muench, 71 (top), 90; *New York Journal-American*, 61, 72; Howard Sochurek, 45; United Nations, 21; University of Wisconsin, Department of Agricultural Journalism, 73.

Copyright© 1968 by Country Beautiful Foundation, Inc. Library of Congress Catalogue Card Number: 68-58164. All rights reserved. This book, or parts thereof, must not be reproduced in any form without permission. Published simultaneously in the Dominion of Canada by Longmans Canada Limited, Toronto. Manufactured in the United States of America. Book design by Wilbur Howe. Color separations, Mueller Color Plate Company.

Contents

B-740

Preface

During a public career that was remarkably long for someone who died so young, Robert F. Kennedy expressed his views on a wide variety of subjects and issues. His public statements, which are excerpted here, show an overriding and constant theme—the exhortation of his fellow citizens to make America a better country, to strive for excellence with noble purpose in every aspect of our national life. He often vigorously defended the United States as it is today, as when he once pointed out bluntly that "Yes, we have our problems in Alabama, but . . . we are not shooting old women and young children in the back as the communists are doing in Berlin."

But there can be no question that in his impatience toward less than the best, he directed his primary attention toward criticizing today's America in the hope of transforming our potential for greatness, as he saw it, into a truly America the beautiful in the future. "A generous and compassionate country—that's what I want this country to stand for, not violence and lawlessness."

The American people responded to him to an exceptional degree, partly because of the crisp eloquence with which he stated his views, but principally because, unlike some men in national political life today who pander to our worst fears and prejudices, Robert Kennedy inspired the best sentiments that are latent in the American people.

While acknowledging the contradictions within the American dream, Robert F. Kennedy held a larger vision of America as compassionate and gentle.

I

The Force of Youth

"To call earlier college eras simply the Silly or Silent Generations was to exaggerate. But I think it fair to describe yours as a generation of unusually genuine and intense concern with social justice and intellectual freedom...."

The young of America and the world felt a particular affinity for Robert F. Kennedy and he for them. In fact, it was this sometimes electrifying aspect of his public career which was emphasized by the mass media during the last months of his life to the point that some critics questioned whether there was substance beneath the charisma. But it was simply a natural consequence of his life and what he believed most deeply.

In the first place, a good case can be made for the contention that the rising idealism and political involvement of the young in the late 1960's had its genesis during the Presidency of John F. Kennedy. This combined with Robert Kennedy's youthful appearance and vigor and his own persistent idealism and obvious political commitment to create this alliance. The hunger of youth for change and their refusal to accept the old complacencies about injustice were matched by Kennedy's own impatience with the status quo and his sensitiveness to the deprivations suffered by others. Kennedy saw the young as a valid social and political force, one that was "going ahead with [its] own revolution" and one that has "history on [its] side."

The qualities of youth — a state of mind rather than a time of life — are needed to make the transition to a "new order."

". . .History will judge you . . . on the extent you have used your gifts to lighten and enrich the lives of others."

11

Above: This generation is one that has been unusually — and genuinely — concerned with problems of social justice and intellectual freedom ". . . but if you would lead this nation, you must use your education to the limits of your ability."
Opposite page: "We, the world's largest younger generation . . . are the only true international community. We are seeking to change the world and we each have our own work to do if we are to succeed."

Above: "I ask for your help . . . if you will give me your hand, I will work for you . . . ."
Left: This display of enthusiasm typifies the appeal Robert Kennedy had for youth.

13

The specific goals of each nation differ, and yet their hopes for the future are so close...

We must meet our problems with imagination and creativity, not with rigid certitudes.

Among all the youth of the world, [American young people] must play a special role. [But] we are only six percent of the world's population, so we cannot right every wrong and we cannot impose our will upon the other ninety-four percent of mankind. . . . We are neither omnipotent nor omniscient.

These are burdens and frustrations associated with your opportunity, with your responsibility. You must accept them with maturity and understanding.

June 6, 1965
State University College
Plattsburgh, New York

14

This is a generation truly concerned...

It's simply not enough for us to send abroad thousands and thousands of nice, good-looking, eager young people. Fourth of July speeches are not enough, either. It is just not true that the United States is a perfectly grand place where everyone loves everyone else.

What these young people need is a real understanding of their own country as well as the rest of the world so they can discuss questions intelligently. It just doesn't make sense to go abroad and tell people there we are getting along with one another at home much better now. Look at Mississippi.

Generalities are no good. If you don't have the answers, I think you're dead. [Urging young people to travel and learn in U.S. first.]

December 5, 1962
Council on Student Travel

To call earlier college eras simply the Silly or Silent Generations was to exaggerate. But I think it fair to describe yours as a generation of unusually genuine and intense concern with social justice and intellectual freedom. . . .

. . . Peace marchers or college civil rights demonstrators may not always express their concern in the wisest or most effective manner, but it is clear that those concerns are deeply felt.

June 7, 1964
Marquette University
Milwaukee, Wisconsin

The nonrecognition of individuality — the sense that no one is listening — is . . . pronounced in our politics. Television, newspapers, magazines, are a cascade of words, official statements, policies, explanations and declarations; all flow from the height of government down to the passive citizen; the young must feel, in their efforts to speak back, like solitary salmon trying to breast Grand Coulee Dam. The words which submerge us, all too often, speak the language of a day irrelevant to our young. And the language of politics is too often insincerity. And if we add to the insincerity, and the absence of dialogue, the absurdity of a politics in which a Byron de la Beckwith can declare as a candidate for Lieutenant Governor of Mississippi, we can understand why so many of our young people have turned from engagement to disengagement.

February 24, 1967
Democratic Action dinner
Philadelphia, Pennsylvania

If you are to help lead this nation, you must use, to the limits of your power, the education you have been given here. This education has taught you the value of fact, and there can be no meaningful politics which is ignorant of the facts.

June 15, 1965
Queens College
Flushing, New York

The Kennedys displayed — and, to the young, symbolized — those qualities of youth demanded by "this swiftly changing planet."

A free mind naturally seeks out reality, even though it may be painful...

I suspect there may always be arguments about what constitutes a higher education, but wise men through the ages have at least been able to agree on its purpose.

Its purpose is not only to discipline and instruct, but above all to *free* the mind — to free it from the darkness, the narrowness, the groundless fears and self-defeating passions of ignorance.

And so perhaps it's not too much to say that what we are celebrating here today is the liberation, the setting free of your minds.

From now on you have earned the right to do your own learning, to develop your own insights and draw your own conclusions, to conduct your own explorations in the life you find around you. Your minds have been freed.

You may sometimes regret it; for a free mind insists on seeking out reality, and reality is often a far more painful matter than the soft and comfortable illusions of the intellectually poor.

But your regret will be nothing compared with your advantage — the measureless advantage you will always have over the vast majority of human beings on this earth.

In the light of a truly freed mind, no prejudice can disguise itself as zeal, no bullying can masquerade as leadership, no pettiness can pose as importance.

The freed mind will never confuse a sentimentality with a true emotion, an act of violence with an act of heroism, a slogan with a cause.

Men and women with freed minds may often be mistaken, but they are seldom fooled. They may be influenced, but they can't be intimidated. They may be perplexed, but they will never be lost.

June 2, 1963
Trinity College
Washington, D.C.

You are the first college to become a major political issue since George III attacked Harvard for being a center of political rebellion and subversion. And he was right.

As for me, I am glad of Berkeley, and I am glad to be here with you. For I am sympathetic, and I welcome the passionate concern with the condition and future of the American nation which can be found on this campus.

That future does not belong to those who are content with today, apathetic toward common problems and man alike, timid and fearful in the face of new ideas and bold projects. Rather it will belong to those who can blend passion, reason and courage in a personal commitment to the ideals and great enterprises of American society. It will belong to those who see that wisdom can only emerge from the clash of contending views, the passionate expression of deep and hostile beliefs. Plato said, "A life without criticism is not worth living." . . .

For it is not enough to allow dissent. We must demand it. For there is much to dissent from.

We dissent from the fact that millions are trapped in poverty while the nation grows rich . . . from the sight of most of mankind living in poverty . . . from cities which blunt our senses and turn the ordinary acts of daily life into a painful struggle . . . from the willful needless destruction of natural pleasure and beauty . . . Yet we must, as thinking men, distinguish between the right of dissent and the way we choose to exercise that right . . .

. . . That dissent which consists simply of sporadic and dramatic acts sustained by neither continuing labor or reason — that dissent which seeks to demolish while lacking both the desire and direction for rebuilding, that dissent which contemptuously or out of laziness casts aside the practical weapons and instruments of change and progress — that kind of dissent is merely self-indulgence. . . .

October 23, 1966
Berkeley campus
University of California

. . . You have been lifted onto a tiny, sunlit island while all around you lies a dark ocean of human misery, injustice, violence, and fear. . . . history will judge you, and, as the years pass, you will ultimately judge yourself on the extent to which you have used your gifts to lighten and enrich the lives of your fellow men.

In your hands, not with Presidents or leaders, is the future of your world, and the fulfillment of the best qualities of your own spirit.

October 23, 1966
Berkeley campus
University of California

". . . You have been lifted onto a tiny, sunlit island while all around you lies a dark ocean of human misery. . .".

As educated persons, we must distinguish between the right of dissent and how we exercise that right.

17

When a hundred student body presidents and editors of college newspapers; hundreds of former Peace Corps volunteers; dozens of present Rhodes Scholars question the basic premises of the [Vietnam] war, they should not and cannot be ignored.

These students oppose the war for the brutality and the horror of all wars, and for the particular terror of this one. But for our young people, I suspect, Vietnam is a shock as it cannot be to us. They did not know World War II, or even Korea. These students . . . are the children not of the Cold War, but of the Thaw. . . . [Vietnam] is surrounded by rhetoric they do not understand or accept. Their memories of communism are not of Stalin's purges and death camps, not even the terrible revelations of the Twentieth Party Congress or the streets of Hungary. They see the world as one in which communist states can be each others' deadliest enemies or even friends of the West, in which communism is certainly no better, but perhaps no worse, than many other evil and repressive dictatorships all around the world — with which we conclude alliances when that is felt to be in our interest.

However the war may seem to us, they see it as one in which the largest and most powerful nation on earth is killing children (they do not care if accidentally) in a remote and insignificant land. We speak of past commitments, of the burden of past mistakes. They ask why they should now atone for mistakes made before many of them were born, before almost any could vote.

February 24, 1967
Americans for Democratic Action dinner
Philadelphia, Pennsylvania

I ask for your help. If you will give me your help, if you will give me your hand, I will work for you and we will have a new America. . . .

Our country is in danger, not just from foreign enemies, but above all from our own misguided policies. There is a contest on, not for the rule of America, but for the heart of America. . . .

I am concerned that at the end of it all there will only be more Americans killed, more of our treasures spilled out; and because of the bitterness and hatred on every side of this war, more hundreds of thousands of Vietnamese slaughtered; so that they may say, as Tacitus said of Rome: "They made a desert and called it peace."

March 18, 1968
Kansas State University
Manhattan, Kansas

Just as my wife and I have a warm feeling for you and your university, so President Kennedy had a warm feeling for Japan. He was looking forward to coming and he was planning to come to your university.

He was more a President of young people than of any other group. Really, what he was attempting to do was to fight the enemies of peace — illiteracy, disease and hunger — around the world.

January 18, 1964
Waseda University
Tokyo, Japan

We stand here in the name of freedom.

At the heart of that western freedom and democracy is the belief that the individual man, the child of God, is the touchstone of value, and all society, groups, the state, exist for his benefit. Therefore, the enlargement of liberty for individual human beings must be the supreme goal and the abiding practice of any Western society. . . .

Each nation has different obstacles and different goals, shaped by the vagaries of history and experience. Yet as I talk to young people around the world I am impressed not by diversity but by the closeness of their goals, their desires and concerns and hope for the future. There is discrimination in New York, apartheid in South Africa and serfdom in the mountains of Peru. People starve in the streets in India; intellectuals go to jail in Russia; thousands are slaughtered in Indonesia; wealth is lavished on armaments everywhere. These are differing evils. But they are the common works of man.

And therefore they call upon common qualities of conscience and of indignation, a shared determination to wipe away the unnecessary sufferings of our fellow human beings at home and particularly around the world.

It demands the qualities of youth: not a time of life but a state of mind, a temper of the will, a quality of the imagination, a predominance of courage over timidity, of the appetite for adventure over the love of ease. . . .

. . . It is young people who must take the lead.

"There is," said an Italian philosopher, "nothing more difficult to take in hand, more perilous to conduct, or more uncertain in its success than to take the lead in the introduction of a new order of things." Yet this is the measure of the task of your generation and the road is strewn with many dangers.

First there is the danger of futility; the belief that there is nothing one man or one woman can do against the enormous array of the world's ills. . . .

. . . [Yet] each time a man stands up for an ideal or acts to improve the lot of others, or strikes out against injustice, he sends forth a tiny ripple of hope, and crossing each other from a million different centers of energy and daring, those ripples build a current that can sweep down the mightiest walls of oppression and resistance.

The second danger is that of practicality; of those who say that hopes and beliefs must bend before immediate necessities. . . .

But if there is one thing President Kennedy stood for that touched the most profound feeling of young people across the world, it was the belief that idealism, high aspirations and deep convictions are not incompatible with the most practical and efficient of programs — that there is no basic inconsistency between ideals and realistic possibilities — no separation between the deepest desires of heart and mind and the rational application of human effort to human problems.

A third danger is timidity. . . . Moral courage is a rarer commodity than bravery in battle or great intelligence. Yet it is the one essential, vital quality for those who seek to change a world which yields most painfully to change. . . .

. . . We are . . . the world's largest younger generation. Each of us has our own work to do.

June 6, 1966
University of Capetown
Capetown, South Africa.

It is the young people who must take the lead...

The purpose of education rests ultimately in liberating the mind from the narrow path of ignorance.

II

America in the World

The Achievement of Peace and Freedom

"The greatest success for nations, as for individuals, is found in truth to themselves. We did not build the United States on anticommunism. . . . Let our emphasis be, then, less on what the communists are doing to threaten peace and order in Latin America—and more on what we can do to help build a better life for its people."

For a man who never held a higher office than Attorney General or United States Senator, Robert F. Kennedy was greeted during his visits to other countries as a full-fledged world leader, as indeed he was in almost any except a formal sense. Of course this was partly due to the great esteem in which President Kennedy was held by people throughout the world. Robert Kennedy called attention to this in Germany in 1964 when he said: ". . . In traveling through my own country, and now in Germany, I have come to understand that the hope President Kennedy kindled is not dead but alive." However, during Robert Kennedy's trips to the Far East, South America, East Africa, Poland, Germany and even South Africa, it became apparent that he was a person to whom people around the world warmly responded because of his own qualities. Between 1963 and his death no other American politician could equal the appeal he had abroad; few international leaders have ever had it.

Robert Kennedy supported a strong international defense system, but believed real peace could only be won through negotiation.

He used his international influence to encourage the growth of freedom, justice and self-determination wherever he went, but he balanced this with the recognition that the revolutionary changes taking place, particularly in former colonies, must not be allowed to endanger world peace. The fostering of nuclear controls to reduce the chance of war he believed to be one of the primary roles of the United States. He also advocated that this nation serve as a source of financial support and know-how for developing nations, and he believed that we should not base such aid on the threat of communism to another country but, more positively, "on what we can do to help build a better life for its people."

On one of the most controversial issues of our time, the Vietnam War, Kennedy changed his mind, and readily admitted that he had done so. In 1965 he said that "I support the effort that's being made by President Johnson." In February 1968 he stated: "The history of conflict among nations does not record another such lengthy and consistent chronicle of error." A little later he warned against the United States playing God and deciding "in Washington, D. C., what cities, what towns, what hamlets in Vietnam are going to be destroyed." A much better way he believed to influence the course of other nations was to set an example at home. "People [in other countries] just . . . . are not going to accept the fact that we believe in the Constitution . . . or the Declaration of Independence if we treat part of our population as inferior human beings."

I know what he [John F. Kennedy] meant when he surveyed the wall of shame and measured it against your courage and said, "Ich bin ein Berliner."

Surrounded by hostility, beseiged by enemies, your freedom in jeopardy, you have emerged from each of these assaults, stronger, greater and more resolute. For this President Kennedy congratulated you, and on behalf of free men everywhere, he thanked you. . .

June 26, 1964
Unveiling memorial plaque
for John F. Kennedy
Berlin, Germany

. . . The man from Pittsburgh is not free until the man from Peiping is free, the man from West Berlin is not free until his brother from East Berlin is also free.

Here on the front line of freedom you serve not only for yourselves and for your country; you defend freedom for my country. You stand with your allies and you defend freedom for free men everywhere. . .

. . . We live in a world of exceptional uncertainty and hazard, but we live in a world that gives us a foundation for a future of exceptional excitement and possibility. That foundation is freedom.

June 26, 1964
Free University of Berlin
Berlin, Germany

This gallant democracy [Israel], this nation of survivors from history's greatest example of man's capacity for senseless cruelty to his fellow men cannot be allowed to succumb to the threats and assaults of her neighbors.

June, 1967
Fordham University
New York, New York

The day is long past when any nation could retreat behind walls of stone or curtains of iron or bamboo.

The winds of freedom and progress and justice blow across the highest battlements, enter at every crevice, are carried by jet planes and communications satellites and by the very air we breathe.

June 8, 1966
Witwatersrand University
Johannesburg, South Africa

I have seen [in Asia] men clambering out of stagnation and squalor and demanding to be admitted to the twentieth century. I have seen a new world beginning to emerge out of centuries of oblivion. Half of the earth is marching out of the darkness into the sunlight.

It is a stirring experience to watch whole nations struggling to achieve political independence and economic growth. It is stirring, and it is significant, because the energies released in this great historic movement — let us not mistake this — are going to reshape the world and determine the future of man.

February 24, 1962
Beethoven Hall
Bonn, Germany

The day is gone when nations can isolate themselves behind a wall...

Opposite page: In a tribute to the courage of Berliners, the former Attorney General lays a wreath at the wall dividing East from West Berlin.

23

Robert Kennedy is greeted by a tumultuous crowd of young South American students.

We built the United States on our strengths, energy and talents...

We are not now meeting our responsibilities. Our economic aid to the rest of the world amounts in total to less than $2 billion — perhaps one-third of one percent of our national income, perhaps one-fifth of one-tenth of what is needed to meet the challenge of this century.

. . . In order to solve the pressing problems of world poverty, developed countries must make a greater contribution — of money and mind, of time and toil. . . . the United States can and must make the greatest share of these contributions.

> June 6, 1965
> State University College
> Plattsburgh, New York

Latin America can speak to the nations of Asia and Africa from the platform of common problems and understanding which we in the United States do not completely share. . . .

. . . Latin-American nations have an opportunity and a responsibility to contribute to the drive for economic advancement and human dignity all over the world. . . .

. . . With the energy and devotion to country I saw everywhere in Latin America, the result in our time must be this continent's having a position of major force and leadership for good in the world.

> November 30, 1965
> National Labor Federation meeting
> Caracas, Venezuela

The greatest success for nations, as for individuals, is found in truth to themselves. We did not build the United States on anti-communism. The strength of our institutions, the energy and talent of Americans, came out of our long struggle to build a nation of justice and freedom and happiness. Ours is the strength of positive faith; we need neither to hate nor fear our adversaries. Let our emphasis be, then, less on what the communists are doing to threaten peace and order in Latin America — and more on what we can do to help build a better life for its people.

> May 9 and 10, 1966
> "The Alliance for Progress:
> Symbol and Substance"
> U. S. Senate

We should not assist those governments which perpetuate privilege and use our aid to prevent reform...

There is a temptation — one to which we have sometimes given in — to use our great power and our aid to force agreement from other nations or to punish them for their disagreement. This temptation is most obvious in matters of foreign policy and the Cold War: whether a country voted in the O.A.S. to approve our action in the Dominican Republic, or perhaps whether it recognizes Communist China or votes for its admission to the United Nations. These are matters of considerable importance to the United States. It is understandable that officials in the Executive branch or members of Congress or others in the country would feel that nations which fail to stand with us are not reliable allies and should not receive U. S. assistance.

But this feeling, so understandable in the passions and excitement of the moment, can only be harmful over the long run. We expect our Government to reflect the feelings of our people. Latin-Americans expect the same from their governments and deeply resent any government which seems less than fully independent in its decisions. One Latin-American president put it to me succinctly: "If you want a government that says always 'yes, yes, yes,' " he told me, "you will soon have to deal with a government that says always, 'no, no, no'."

We must turn our attention to helping our Latin American neighbors build a better life.

Increased economic aid to underdeveloped nations is a positive measure against communism.

May 9 and 10, 1966
"The Alliance for Progress:
Symbol and Substance"
U. S. Senate

This we must clearly understand: Communism is not a native growth in Latin America. Given any meaningful alternative, its people will reject communism and follow the path of democratic reform and membership in the inter-American system. But if we allow ourselves to become allied with those to whom the cry of "communism!" is only an excuse for the perpetuation of privilege — if we assist, with military material and other aid, governments which use that aid to prevent reform for their people — then we will give the communists a strength which they cannot attain by anything they themselves might do.

President Johnson's Mexico City address set what must be our policy: "We will not be deterred," he said, "by those who say that to risk change is to risk communism."

May 9 and 10, 1966
"The Alliance for Progress:
Symbol and Substance"
U. S. Senate

25

Today's world is one of continuing change...

Twenty-five years ago today with the invasion of Poland, the most evil men in history unleashed the most destructive war in history. It is America's responsibility to do all that it can to walk the final mile to make sure that that never happens again.

Wherever I have traveled in the last year, I have found confidence in the United States. We have increased our strength and used it with wisdom and restraint. The peace is more secure because we have used our strength to serve its cause. This must be continued.

But there is much much more that we need to do. The world is full of hungry people, of men in search of dignity, of people who cry out to escape from the grinding cycle of poverty in which their ancestors have been trapped since time began.

We must act to keep their faith and freedom. If we cannot help them now, we will not long be able to help ourselves. . .

. . . The principles in which we believe are too important to take for granted, too precious to be lost through indecision or through apathy.

September 1, 1964
Acceptance speech for nomination
by New York Democratic Convention
for the U. S. Senate

[About reconciliation of Eastern and Western Europe and an end to international tensions.]

Just because we cannot see clearly the end of the road, that is no reason for not setting out on the essential journey. On the contrary, great change dominates the world, and unless we move with change we will become its victim.

July 1, 1964
Farewell statement
Warsaw, Poland

Nuclear capability, then, will soon lie within the grasp of the many. And it is all too likely that if events continue on their present course, this technical capability will be used to produce nuclear weapons. . . .

. . . Once nuclear war were to start, even between small remote countries, it would be exceedingly difficult to stop a step-by-step progression of local war into a general conflagration.

Eighty million Americans — and hundreds of millions of other people — would die within the first twenty-four hours of a full-scale nuclear exchange. And as Chairman Khrushchev once said, the survivors would envy the dead.

This is not an acceptable future. We owe it to ourselves, to our children, to our forebears and our posterity, to prevent such a holocaust. But the proliferation of nuclear weapons immensely increases the chances that the world might stumble into catastrophe.

. . . It is clear, in short, that the United States — and the entire world — have the most vital interest in preventing the scattering of nuclear weapons. Upon the success of this effort depends the only future our children will have.

The United States is stronger than almost any other nation and so has the greater responsibility in the effort to control nuclear weapons.

". . . But we have not yet taken the second step. The world has not moved beyond the limited nuclear test-ban itself. . . . If we are to leave our children a planet in which to live safely, to fulfill the bright promise of their lives, we must resume the journey to peace."

The need to halt the spread of nuclear weapons must be a central priority of American policy. Of all our major interests, this now deserves and demands the greatest additional effort. This is a broad statement, for our interests are broad. The need to be strong — to meet aggression in far-off places — to work closely with allies all over the world — all these needs must be met. And the crises of the moment often pose urgent questions of grave importance for national security. But these immediate problems, and others like them, have been with us constantly for twenty years — and will be with us far into the future. Should nuclear weapons become generally available to the world, however, each crisis of the moment might well become the last crisis for all mankind.

Thus, none of the momentary crises are more than small parts of the larger question of whether our politics can grow up to our technology. . . .

. . . The United States took the initiative and made maximum effort to secure the nuclear test-ban treaty in 1963. . . .

. . . But we have not yet taken the second step. The world has not moved beyond the limited nuclear test-ban itself to halt the proliferation of nuclear weapons. If we are to leave our children a planet in which to live safely, to fulfill the bright promise of their lives, we must resume the journey toward peace.

It is necessary that our politics reach and grow to match our technology...

27

Robert Kennedy, in 1965, supported President Johnson's policy on the war in Vietnam.

We should take the first, the best, and the ultimate steps to control arms...

. . . There have been suggestions that the chief stumbling block to such a treaty is the war in Vietnam. But wholly apart from the strains resulting from that war, I think we have not ourselves done all we can to secure a non-proliferation treaty. . . .

. . . In all our efforts — we will have to deal with one of the most perplexing and difficult questions affecting American foreign policy: China. It is difficult to negotiate on any question with the intransigent leaders of Communist China. And it is doubly difficult when we are engaged in South Vietnam. China is profoundly suspicious of and hostile to us — as we are highly suspicious of her. . . . But China is there. China will have nuclear weapons. And without her participation it will be infinitely more difficult, perhaps impossible in the long run, to prevent nuclear proliferation. . . .

. . . At an appropriate time and in an appropriate manner, therefore, we should vigorously pursue negotiations on this subject with China. But if we must ultimately have the cooperation of China and the Soviet Union and France and all other nations with any nuclear capability whatever, it does not follow that we should wait for that cooperation before beginning our efforts.

We are stronger — and therefore have more responsibility — than any nation on earth; we should make the first effort — the greatest effort — and the last effort — to control nuclear weapons. We can and must begin immediately. . .

. . . It is only by study and actions, by general concern throughout the government, that the problem of nuclear proliferation will remain where it belongs — in our constant attention, the object of our principal concern. And we can and must continue to re-examine our own attitudes — to insure that we do not lapse back into the fatalistic and defeatist belief that war is inevitable, or that our course is too fixed to be affected by what we do. . . .

Above all, we must recognize what is at stake. We must face realities — however unpleasant the sight, however difficult the challenge they pose us. And we must realize that peace is not inaction, nor the mere absence of war. "Peace," said President Kennedy, "is a process — a way of solving problems." It is only as we devote our every effort to the solution of these problems that we are at peace; it is only if we succeed that there will be peace for our children.

June 23, 1965
U. S. Senate debate on nuclear
proliferation

We must realize that Vietnam has become more and more an open military conflict . . . in which military action on our part is essential just to allow the Government to act politically.

What I say today is in the hope that the lessons of the last twenty years will be applied in other places — so that we are able to win these wars before they reach the stage of all-out military conflict now apparent in South Vietnam.

I think the history of the last twenty years demonstrates beyond doubt that our approach to revolutionary war must be political — political first, political last, political always.

Where the needs and grievances of the people begin to be met by the political process, insurgency loses its popular character and becomes a police problem — as it did in Venezuela and Colombia, in the Philippines and Malaya.

July 9, 1965
International Police Academy
Washington, D. C.

I support the effort that's being made in Vietnam by President Johnson. I believe this to be most important. If the effort in Vietnam becomes merely a military effort, we shall win some of the battles, but we will lose the over-all struggle. The people of Vietnam need to feel that their future should rest with Saigon and not Hanoi.

We need to give them security — that is going to require police and military action — but at the same time, social, political, economic, educational and agricultural progress has to be made for the peasants of that tragic land. And we need to do much in that field.

August 25, 1965

There is need to make progress in the quality of life for the peasant in Vietnam...

By 1968, the Senator was urging a revision of the Vietnam war policy with an emphasis on developing the land.

29

*Do not curse the past
but use it to
enlighten the future...*

We have made a military commitment in Southeast Asia, but will we now have the imagination and the initiative to develop a program which will not just take lives but save them?

We have spoken out against inhuman slaughters perpetrated by the Nazis and the communists, but will we speak out also against the inhuman slaughter in Indonesia, where over 100,000 alleged communists have been not perpetrators, but victims?

February 7, 1966
Utica, New York

We must learn, whether in Southeast Europe or Southeast Asia, to deal with nations not as part of a monolithic communist movement which no longer exists, not as tools of far-away capitals which cannot control them, but as nations whose significance and possible danger to our own national security must be carefully weighed on a case-by-case basis.

April 13, 1968
Charleston, West Virginia

For the sake of those young Americans who are fighting today, if for no other reason, the time has come to take a new look at the war in Vietnam; not by cursing the past but by using it to illuminate the future.

And the first and necessary step is to face the facts. It is to seek out the austere and painful reality of Vietnam; freed from wishful thinking, false hopes and sentimental dreams. It is to rid ourselves of the "good company" of those illusions which have lured us into the deepening swamp of Vietnam.

[The fact that there are no secure enclaves] has not happened because all men are not brave or effective, because they are. It is because we have misconceived the nature of the war. It is because we have sought to resolve by military might a conflict whose issue depends upon the will and conviction of the South Vietnamese people. It is like sending a lion to halt an epidemic of jungle rot. . . .

Reality is grim and painful. But it is only a remote echo of the anguish toward which a policy founded on illusion is surely taking us. This is a great nation and a strong people. Any who seek to comfort rather than speak plainly, reassure rather than instruct, promise satisfaction rather than reveal frustration — they deny that greatness and drain that strength. For today as it was in the beginning, it is the truth that makes us free.

February 8, 1968
Chicago, Illinois

The history of conflict among nations does not record another such lengthy and consistent chronicle of error [as in Vietnam].

It is time for the truth. It is time to face the reality that a military victory is not in sight and that it probably never will come.

February 8, 1968
Chicago, Illinois

*Opposite page: Through the Peace Corps, it is possible
to free many people from the grinding cycle of poverty.*

These peasants of Vietnam cannot be left with a desert. Because peace is neither inaction nor the mere absence of war, we have a responsibility in Vietnam to make progress now in the social, political, economic, educational, and agricultural life of the country.

Right: "It is time to face the reality that a military victory is not in sight."

Below: [This war] "is like sending a lion to halt an epidemic of jungle rot."

Because minority groups have common problems and a mutual understanding, they can lead in the drive for human dignity.

Half of the world is marching into sunlight...

Every American knows in his heart the truth of the democratic way of life. But a nice warm feeling in the heart doesn't take the place of knowing what you are talking about. There is no shortage abroad of questions — often belligerent — about American life. Americans who go abroad should do so with a sense of responsibility for providing full and factual answers. . . .

There is no point in trying to make the United States out to be a country without faults, where everything is fine between labor and management, where there are no civil rights difficulties, and where we have no unemployment problems. This kind of approach simply will not be accepted. Students abroad must discuss our problems intelligently, admit our problems, and must say what we are trying to do about them. This is, after all, one of our country's great strengths — we admit our problems but we try to take action to solve them and face up to our responsibilities.

The need is to be candid about our problems and to be informed on what we're doing about them. Unlike the highly trained communist infiltrators and propagandists, we have no "party line" in this country. Nor is there need of one. The facts — as opposed to the stereotypes exploited by our adversaries — will speak for themselves.

February 16, 1963
"A Free Trade in Ideas"
from *Saturday Review*

Do we have the moral right to decide in the United States what villages will be destroyed in Vietnam?

. . . There is a question of our moral responsibility. Are we like the God of the Old Testament that we can decide, in Washington, D.C., what cities, what towns, what hamlets in Vietnam are going to be destroyed? Is it because we think it may possibly protect the people of Thailand, the people of Malaysia, the people of Hawaii, or keep certain people out of Texas or California or Massachusetts or New York?

Or do we have that authority to kill tens and tens of thousands of people because we have a commitment to the South Vietnamese people?

I question whether we have that right in this country.

March 7, 1968
Vietnam debate
U. S. Senate

We all know the truth of the democratic way of life,
and we must face its weaknesses with candor.

"We must face realities . . . . It is only as we devote our every effort to the solution of these problems that we are at peace; it is only if we succeed that there will be peace for our children."

The contributions that a free press makes in these countries around the world is overwhelming. . . Despite all the effort that's made by your organization and the effort that is made by the U.S.I.A., by the Voice of America, and by many others to bring the truth to many of these countries, I was overwhelmed by the lack of understanding, the misinformation, that exists in many of these countries throughout the world that we visited.

So we have this tremendous problem of misunderstanding and misinformation. There is a great warmth in all of these countries toward the United States. . . And it brings home to me what a great, what a major difference it makes to what we do here in the United States and what an effect that has in all of these countries around the globe.

And I think of this in my own department, the Department of Justice, and the problems and struggles that we are now facing in the field of civil rights. There wasn't one area of the world that I visited whether it was a press conference or a student group or a labor group or business men with whom I visited, that I wasn't asked about civil rights.

Carlos Romulo, before he left Washington, came to see me. We had a short visit. And he said unless we are able to continue to move ahead in this field [civil rights] here in the United States, we cannot possibly win in the struggle with communism throughout the world, because people just are not going to believe or are not going to accept the fact that we believe in the Constitution of the United States or the Declaration of Independence if we treat part of our population as inferior human beings.

April 23, 1962
Associated Press luncheon
New York, New York

We've made progress [against racketeering], but there is still so much to be done because crime is increasing in the United States — crime and juvenile delinquency — four times as fast as our population. And this gets across . . . to the other peoples of the world — that we are a selfish system of government, that all that we are interested in is ourselves, that we are not interested in one another — and that is the picture that is getting across in the definition of capitalism in all of these countries.

. . . We have so much more to offer in all of these countries . . . that we can get across, . . . of the contributions that are made by ordinary citizens to their neighbor; the contributions that are made by charitable organizations to help and assist those who cannot help themselves; the help and assistance that comes from the Federal Government to our citizens who are not able to help themselves. And I think that if we can get these kinds of things across, it's going to make a major difference. The next ten years are going to be the crucial years. If we can move ahead and get people . . . who know and who are experts on American history and know our own system — to go across into these other countries and give talks and lectures — not just propaganda — to go in and admit where we've made mistakes, but show what kind of a system of government that we have here in the United States, which believes in individual freedom and believes that the state exists for the individual, not the individual for the state.

If we can have and set up in all of these countries a peace corps of young people who are willing to join with the young people of this country to go to other lands which are less fortunate to help and assist in this fight for peace, I think that we can make great progress. . . .

April 23, 1962
Associated Press luncheon
New York, New York

Let us send abroad young people who know and understand our history...

American students abroad must be willing and able to discuss our nation's problems intelligently.

III

The Law and Liberty

"The experiences of the last year have strength-ened my belief that despite the efforts of a small minority, the people in the United States are law-abiding people who wish to live by the law, do not want to circumvent court decisions, and are op-posed to actions which will result in violence."

Robert F. Kennedy was educated and trained as a lawyer, but upon graduation from the University of Virginia Law School in 1951 he took a post with the Justice Department rather than becoming a practitioner of law primarily concerned with winning cases and furthering the interests of clients. Thus, from the beginning, Kennedy saw the law as a means through which he could serve the larger purposes of society, as an essential tool for maintaining and creating a just and viable society. During the 1950's, however, Kennedy did not always seem to under-stand that the so-called niceties of the law, such as the Fifth Amend-ment, were there to be observed for guilty and innocent alike. It was during the latter part of this period, as chief counsel for Senator John McClellan's Senate Select Committee on Improper Activities in the Labor and Management Field, that he acquired his reputation for ruthlessness. His merciless questioning of unfriendly witnesses was called "vindictive battering" by one civil libertarian, a Yale law professor.

By the time he was appointed Attorney General by President John F. Kennedy in 1961, Robert Kennedy seemed to have a broadened ap-preciation of the full majesty of the law as a protector of rights as well as a punisher of wrong-doing. He foreshadowed later Supreme Court decisions when he said, also in 1961, that we must "try to help and assist the unfortunate who perhaps cannot pay for attorneys or ap-peals." His tenacity in carrying out the full import of Federal law helped to bring about substantial progress in civil rights in the South while he was in this office, for he believed that law was "both the guardian and the agent of freedom." He also believed that "the decisions of courts, however much we might disagree with them . . . must be followed and respected," for in 1961, he foresaw, that "incidents [such as Little Rock] undermined respect for law and order." However, he probably stated his understanding of the essential place of law in a democracy most succinctly when he said that "our liberties depend upon our respect for law."

The United States Supreme Court building bears the legend "Equal justice under the law," a principle for which Robert Kennedy fought as Attorney General in the Kennedy Administration.

39

I feel strongly about crime wherever it exists...

I think that it is of equal importance to successfully prosecute a case. It is equally important to have examined the facts and determined that there is no prosecution that is necessary. All of these matters are going to be examined objectively.

I think that there are certain inequities that must be studied. I think that there are great advantages in this whole field for the people with greater wealth over the people that are not as well off, and I expect, I know, we are going to study that whole matter to try to help and assist the unfortunate who perhaps cannot pay for attorneys, cannot pay for appeals, cannot pay for appeals all the way to the Supreme Court.

So I think that that is incumbent upon us in the Department of Justice, and we are going to take some steps in order to help and assist these people. I feel very strongly, Senator, about corruption and dishonesty and organized crime. . . . I have a strong feeling against corruption and dishonesty where we find it.

I think that this is a very serious matter now facing the United States, this whole question of organized crime, of gangsters and hoodlums . . . and I will tell you that we are going to pursue all of those matters to the full vigor of the Department of Justice.

[Reply during Senate hearings on his nomination for post of Attorney General to a question about motives and principles involved in making decisions in that office.]

January 13, 1961

Far too much of our police work is spent combating ills which the police cannot effectively fight. Clearly, we cannot permit those who are addicts or alcoholics to threaten our safety and our property. Clearly, we must free the urban citizen from this fear of sick men. But just as clearly we cannot simply put these men in jail, only to have them return to their habits and their crimes.

January 19, 1968
Yonkers, New York

Policemen have the difficult, but necessary task of suspending their prejudice when it appears to be in conflict with the law.

One of the chief attributes of a good lawyer is courage to stand up for the basic ideal of respect for the law...

Victory in a revolutionary war is won not by escalation but by de-escalation. . . .

. . . A government cannot make war on its own people, cannot destroy its own country. To do so is to abandon its reason for existence — its responsibility to its people — and its claim to their allegiance.

Suppose, for example, that a government force is fired upon from a village, or that rebels have forced the village to fly the insurgent flag. A government which attacks that village from the air, or with heavy artillery, abandons all pretense of protecting the people of the village — abandons the first duty of any government worthy of the name. . . .

. . . If all a government can promise its people, in response to insurgent activity, is ten years of napalm and heavy artillery, it will not be a government for long.

> July 9, 1965
> International Police Academy
> Washington, D. C

I think we can understand the father of a child who is slowly dying from malnutrition — and there are children like that in the country today — if he questions what allegiance he owes to the laws of a system that permits that to happen.

> January 16, 1968
> Buffalo, New York

. . . Courage is the most important attribute of a lawyer. . . .

One of my great disappointments in our present efforts to deal with the situation in Mississippi has been the absence of any expression of support from the many distinguished lawyers of that state. I realize in that difficult social situation that to defend the fundamental principles of respect for the law and compliance with Federal court orders would be unpopular and require great courage.

I also understand that many of them may not agree with the decision in Brown vs. the Board of Education [Supreme Court decision-1954-banning school segregation]. But whether they agree or not, they still have their obligations as lawyers and they remain silent.

However, I might also note that there have been no pronouncements in this matter by the American Bar Association.

> September 29, 1962
> University of San Francisco Law School
> San Francisco, California

Black and white together warmly responded to Senator Kennedy during a campaign tour of Indiana.

Above: When one sees the effects of ghetto life on a child, it is easier to understand why many object to the laws of a system that permits this.

Left: "... No citizens can be said to have a heavier stake in this country than American Negroes."

Lawyers have conveniently, perhaps lazily, abdicated responsibility for dealing with major social problems to other professions — to sociologists, educators, community organizers, social workers, psychologists.

. . . We as a profession have backed away from dealing with that larger helplessness [of the indigent].

We have secured the acquittal of an indigent person — but only to abandon him to eviction notices, wage attachments, repossession of goods and termination of welfare benefits.

. . . As it is now, rarely if ever do the best lawyers and the best law firms work with the legal problems that beset the most deprived segments of our society.

. . . What we require is to make law both the guardian and the agent of freedom.

Our professional mandate goes far beyond protecting the presumption of innocence throughout a criminal trial. Our obligation extends to championing a larger presumption — the presumption of individual sanctity and worth which must attend all, rich and poor alike, if the rule is to prevail in reality as it does in Law Day speeches.

> May 1, 1964
> Law Day
> University of Chicago Law School
> Chicago, Illinois

We cannot expect that our problems in connection with civil rights in the South will be solved without discord and disagreement. But we do have a right to expect that local law-enforcement officers will do their jobs at all times, that they will preserve law and order. . . .

> June 7, 1961
> FBI National Academy
> Washington, D. C.

We, the American people, must avoid another Little Rock or another New Orleans. We cannot afford them. It is not only that such incidents do incalculable harm to the children involved and to the relations among people. It is not only that such convulsions seriously undermine respect for law and order and cause serious economic and moral damage. Such incidents hurt our country in the eyes of the world. . . .

For on this generation of Americans falls the full burden of proving to the world that we really mean it when we say all men are created free and are equal before the law. All of us might wish at times that we lived in a more tranquil world, but we don't. And if our times are difficult and perplexing, so are they challenging and filled with opportunity.

To the South, perhaps more than any other section of the country, has been given the opportunity and the challenge and the responsibility of demonstrating America at its greatest — at its full potential of liberty under law.

> May 6, 1961
> Law Day
> University of Georgia
> Athens, Georgia

Surrounded by his aides and supporters, Robert Kennedy tours a Negro district during the California Presidential Primary campaign.

For generations, Americans have prided themselves on being a people with democratic ideals, a people who pay no attention to a man's race, creed, or color. This very phrase has become a truism. But it is a truism with a fundamental defect: It has not been true.

It was the British historian, Lord Acton, who wrote that "laws should be adapted to those who have the heaviest stake in the country, for whom misgovernment means . . . want and pain and degradation and risk to their own lives and to their children's souls."

As Americans, I don't see how any of us can fail to agree with that statement, and surely, by that definition, no citizens can be said to have a heavier stake in this country than American Negroes.

> July 1, 1963
> Senate Commerce Committee
> Hearing on Public Accommodations Bill.

Every day of delay aggravates the problems of discrimination by hardening resentments and undermining confidence in the possibility of legal and peaceful solutions.

> October 15, 1963

The American people cannot afford to have another Little Rock or New Orleans...

43

This government depends upon the full participation of all of its citizens...

... Man has had to struggle to create a system of law and of government in which fundamental freedoms would be linked with the enforcement of justice. We know that we cannot live together without rules which tell us what is right and what is wrong, what is permitted and what is prohibited. We know that it is law which enables men to live together, that creates order out of chaos. We know that law is the glue that holds civilization together.

And we know that if one man's rights are denied, the rights of all are endangered. In our country, the courts have a most important role in safeguarding these rights. The decisions of the courts, however much we might disagree with them, in the final analysis must be followed and respected. If we disagree with a court decision and thereafter, irresponsibly assail the court and defy its rulings, we challenge the foundations of our society.

... The time has long since passed when the people of the United States can be apathetic about their belief and respect for the law and about the necessity of placing our own house in order. As we turn to meet our enemy [communism], to look him full in the face, we cannot afford feet of clay or an arm of glass.

The hardest problems of all in law enforcement are those involving a conflict of law and local customs. History has recorded many occasions when the moral sense of a nation produced judicial decisions . . . . which required difficult local adjustments. The time has long since arrived when loyal Americans must measure the impact of their actions beyond the limits of their own towns or states. For instance, we must be quite aware of the fact that fifty percent of the countries in the United Nations are not white; that around the world, in Africa, South America and Asia, people whose skins are a different color than ours are on the move to gain their measure of freedom and liberty.

From the Congo to Cuba, from South Vietnam to Algiers, in India, Brazil and Iran, men and women and children are straightening their backs and listening — to the evil promises of communist tyranny and the honorable promises of Anglo-American liberty. And these people will decide not only their own future but ours — how the cause of freedom fares in the world.

In the United Nations we are striving to establish a rule of law instead of a rule of force. In that forum and elsewhere around the world, our deeds will speak to us.

You have shown to all the world that we Americans are moving forward together — solving this [racial] problem — under the rule of law.

An integral part of all this is that we make a total effort to guarantee the ballot to every American of voting age — in the North, as well as in the South. The right to vote is the easiest of all rights to grant. The spirit of our democracy, the letter of our Constitution and our laws require that there be no further delay in the achievement of full freedom to vote for all. Our system depends upon the fullest participation of its citizens.

May 6, 1961
Law Day
University of Georgia
Athens, Georgia

"On this generation of Americans falls the full burden of proving to the world that we really mean it when we say that all men are created free and are equal before the law. . . . There can be no further delay. . . ."

Every American has the duty to obey the laws and the right to expect that these laws will be enforced.

It is fundamental in our system that there be respect for the law and compliance with all laws — not just those with which we happen to agree.

[Statement after James Meredith was refused entry to the University of Mississippi.]

September 27, 1962

The experiences of the last year have strengthened my belief that despite the efforts of a small minority, the people in the United States are law-abiding people who wish to live by the law, do not want to circumvent court decisions, and are opposed to actions which will result in violence. I am confident, therefore, that this year's progress will continue, and that it will be carried forward with the effort and approval of the vast majority of the American people.

December 28, 1961
Department of Justice Report to
President John F. Kennedy on
civil rights progress

But all the high rhetoric on Law Day about the noble mansions of the law, all the high-sounding speeches about liberty and justice are meaningless unless people — you and I — breathe meaning and force into it. For our liberties depend upon our respect for the law.

May 6, 1961
Law Day
University of Georgia
Athens, Georgia

People give noble laws their meaning and force...

IV

Man and His Dignity

"Those of us who are white can only dimly guess at what the pain of racial discrimination must be—what it must be like to be turned away from a public place or made to use only a segregated portion of that place, for no reason other than the color of one's skin....

"How can a Negro father explain this intolerable situation to his children? And how can the children be expected to grow up with any sense of pride in being Americans?"

If any one concept can be said to be at the core of all Robert F. Kennedy said and did, it is that nothing is essentially more important than the dignity of each and every individual human being. He dedicated most of his adult life to trying to foster the pre-conditions necessary to the full realization of that dignity: sufficient food and shelter; an environment that provides for more than physical survival and allows for the development of inborn abilities; the opportunity to work, to go to school, and to function generally in society on a basis commensurate with one's talents and ambition; and to be treated with the basic respect due every man whatever his abilities. All of this has been said by other men in America and other places, but few devoted so much energy and passion during the years they lived in attempting to bring these things about in the face of the considerable forces of selfishness, blindness and timidity which constantly resist the building of a just society.

It was a source of amazement to some that someone so well born could seemingly identify so closely with the dispossessed of our society—the black, the poor, the Mexican-American, the American Indian. The cynical saw in it mere political opportunism, but no one could demonstrate how Robert Kennedy's deep concern over the Indian could win him many votes. Perhaps the best indication of the depth of his understanding of the problems of the depressed minorities was that he knew that ultimately he could not put himself in their shoes. "Those of us who are white can only dimly guess. . . ." he said. And he knew that "men need these helpers [psychiatrists and social workers] far less than they need the chance to contribute to themselves, their families and their community—to stand with pride in themselves and with respect among their fellows."

Opposite page: Those who preach about states' rights today are seeking to exploit the individual and deny some the right to be human.

Senator Kennedy strolls over for a visit with students at an integrated school in Portland, Oregon.

Those of us who are white can only dimly guess at what the pain of racial discrimination must be — what it must be like to be turned away from a public place or made to use only a segregated portion of that place, for no reason other than the color of one's skin.

Prostitutes, criminals, communist and fascist conspirators — these people are free to go to the movies and to choose their own seats, as long as they are white.

How can a Negro father explain this intolerable situation to his children? And how can the children be expected to grow up with any sense of pride in being Americans?

October 28, 1963
Annual Convention of the
Theatre Owners of America
New York, New York

Discrimination and prejudice are not worthy of a free nation...

. . . It is difficult to live in the shadow of a multimillion-dollar freeway, to watch the white faces blur as they speed by the problems of the city, returning each evening to the pleasant green lawns of the suburbs.

And it must be difficult beyond measure to share in America's affluence enough to own a television set and to see on that set the hate and fear and ugliness of little Negro children being beaten and clubbed by hoodlums and thugs in Mississippi. . . .

If we deny a man his place in the larger community then he may turn inside to find his manhood and identity, rejecting those he feels have rejected him.

Therefore, far more impressive than the violence of a few is the fact that the overwhelming majority of American Negroes retain the possibilities of peaceful progress within the ordered framework of American politics and life. . . .

October 23, 1966
Berkeley campus
University of California

48

I think we have to develop meaningful programs for housing, employment, education. I think the poverty program is important. I think the new housing program and the recent education bill are all of great significance. Basically, I think that we have to give people, particularly the young people, some hope for the future, some indication that there is some meaning in our society which makes it worthwhile for them to support that society.

[In response to the question: "What needs to be done to prevent . . . outbreaks . . . such as in Los Angeles?"]

August 25, 1965

In spite of the recent violence, the vast majority of American Negroes desire equality through peaceful means.

The problem that is Watts — and Harlem and Bedford-Stuyvesant and South Chicago and North Philadelphia — is not one that will yield to laws protecting legal rights.

It is the kind of problem that will yield only to other kinds of fundamental change — to the forces created by better education and better housing and better job opportunities.

And it will yield only when the people of the ghetto acquire and wisely exercise political power in the community, only when they are able to establish meaningful communication with a society from which they have been excluded up to now.

The American Negro — already a nation apart for 300 years — is now physically separated from the rest of society by a situation of segregation unparalleled in our country's history. In the great urban areas, he lives in a vast slum where from his birth to his death he enjoys all the privileges of second-class citizenship. Whatever the issue — be it job opportunities, educational facilities, housing, parks, or health care — he comes off second best. . . .

The Negro's frustration about these conditions and about the massive indifference with which the rest of society had reacted to them was what boiled to the surface in Watts.

The question now is whether we really did learn anything from Watts — and from Rochester and Harlem and North Philadelphia.

April 19, 1966
Kerhonkson, New York

Robert Kennedy's concern for children was seen in the unique rapport he could establish with the young.

Surely we don't need a new court decision to tell us that the Negro is entitled to decent housing, to equal opportunities in employment, or equal opportunities to advance from unskilled into skilled and responsible jobs . . . . the Constitution points the way clearly to what thinking Americans have known all along: That racial discrimination is not worthy of us; that the stifling air of prejudice is not fit to be breathed by the people of a nation that takes pride in calling itself free. . . . Shameful scenes of riot and bloodshed are outward manifestations of an inner disease. . . .

Let no white Northerner delude himself that discrimination is chiefly a matter of Southern concern. It may be true that a Northern Negro is free to register at a Hilton Hotel, but how much pride or pleasure can he take in this when he can't buy three meals a day for his children?

June 21, 1963
175th Anniversary of Ratification
of Constitution
Independence Mall
Philadelphia, Pennsylvania

49

*T*oo often the cry of states' rights is a denial of American rights...

"The civil rights issue is not a popularity contest. The job must be done because it is right, and it will be done."

Senator Kennedy saw the dignity of each person he encountered; to him, nothing was as important as protecting that dignity.

*I*t makes no sense that we should ask military personnel to make sacrifices and serve away from home and at the same time see their children treated as inferiors by local requirements that they attend segregated schools.

It is made even more incongruous considering that these school systems are supported by public funds, contributed in part by the fathers of these children.

September 17, 1962
Suit to end segregation in public
schools receiving Federal aid
Prince George County, Virginia

*S*tates' rights, as our forefathers conceived it, was a protection of the right of the individual citizen. Those who preach most frequently about states' rights today are not those seeking the protection of the individual citizen, but his exploitation.

The time is long past — if indeed it ever existed — when we should permit the noble concept of states' rights to be betrayed and corrupted into a slogan to hide the bold denial of American rights, of civil rights, and of human rights.

July 18, 1963
Hearing on civil rights bill
Senate Judiciary Committee

This country and the Federal Government are not going back on the progress we have made...

We have made significant progress in enforcing the Civil Rights Acts of 1957 and 1960. . . . As a result of this action, thousands of Negro citizens have been enabled to enjoy the franchise which is rightfully theirs. However . . . we have become keenly aware of certain obstacles to fully, effectively use the law.

. . . There is no such thing as retroactive voting. Once an election date is past, the disenfranchised citizen has suffered a loss which is irreparable. No amount of subsequent litigation can repair the damage done to such citizens or to the integrity of our democratic system.

. . . One white gentleman interpreted that section [Title I literacy test qualification] in the words: "I think that a Neogroe Should Have 8 years in college Be fore voting Becouse he don't under Stand." He was registered.

June 26, 1963
House Judiciary Committee
Hearing on civil rights
legislation

If we fail to act promptly and wisely at this crucial point in our history, grave doubts will be thrown on the very premise of American democracy.

If we enact a program that presents a reasonable opportunity for the Negroes to resolve their legitimate grievances — only then will this nation be living up to its ideals.

. . . This bill [civil rights] springs from the people's desire to correct a wrong that has been allowed to exist too long in our society. It comes from the basic sense of justice in the hearts of all Americans.

June 26, 1963
House Judiciary Committee
Hearing on civil rights
legislation

These decisions [civil rights legislation] are not going to be changed. This country is not going back to a time when a woman could die in the street because a state law would not let a person of her color into the local hospital. It is not going back to a time when Negroes were barred from voting and the Federal Government did nothing about it.

September 20, 1964
Free Synagogue of Westchester
County,
Mt. Vernon, New York

"In the great urban areas, [the Negro] lives in a vast slum where . . . he enjoys the privileges of second-class citizenship."

Around the world, freedom's cause will be judged by civil rights progress here.

In the North the civil rights problems are more complex and so more violence may occur there than in the South...

"We can never move too fast by giving men the liberty they were guaranteed a century ago. . . ."

There's no question that in the next thirty or forty years, a Negro can also achieve the same position that my brother has as President of the United States, certainly within that period of time.

It's a matter [attacks on Negroes] that disturbs us tremendously, but I think that people should also understand some of the good things that are being done in this area [civil rights], that this doesn't really represent the American people or the American Government, that this is just a small minority group which is causing these problems and difficulties.

It doesn't represent the vast majority of the people in the South, this kind of riot, this kind of lawlessness, and it certainly doesn't represent the feelings of the United States Government or the American people. That is why we took the steps that we took to try to prevent it, and we have prevented it . . . I am not saying to you, and I would be less than frank if I did, that these kinds of events are ended now and that they won't have any racial prejudice or violence of the future, because we will have them. But we are not going to accept the "status quo" in the matter of Negro rights.

May 26, 1961
Broadcast over Voice of America

There's a revolution going on in the United States, and people don't like their lives upset. But the civil rights issue is not a popularity contest. The job must be done because it is right and it will be done.

May 1, 1964
University of Chicago Law School
Chicago, Illinois

I don't think [the civil rights movement is] necessarily entering a new phase. It should have been anticipated that we were going to have many difficulties. . .

In many ways the North has more difficult and complex problems than the South. Solutions are more difficult. Furthermore, the make-up of the movement is far different from what it is in the South. It lacks the religious overtones and it lacks the leadership that the Southern civil rights movement has. The fact that the problems are more difficult and complex in the North suggests more violence may occur in the North.

August 25, 1965

That [Negro] revolution has now entered a new stage, one that is at once more hopeful and more difficult, more important and more painful. It is the effort to enforce newly won rights and give them content. . . . in the face of the ominous growth of renewed hostility among the races. . . .

Some of us say the Negro has made great progress, which is true — and that he should be satisfied and patient — which is neither true nor realistic. In the past twenty years we have witnessed a revolution of rising expectations in almost every continent. That revolution has spread to the Negro nation confined within our own. . . .

But if any man claims the Negro should be content or satisfied, let him say he would willingly change the color of his skin and go to live in the Negro section of a large city. Then, and only then, has he a right to such a claim.

Yet, however much the condition of most Negroes must call forth compassion, the violence of a few demands condemnation and action. . . . Still far more disturbing than the chaotic, self-destructive violence of Watts or Oakland are the statements of a very few Negro spokesmen . . . who have called for hatred to fight prejudice, racism to meet racism, violence to destroy oppression.

Here is the seat of tragedy for black and white alike. . . .

It would be a national disaster to permit resentment or fear at the actions of a few to drive increasing numbers of white and black Americans into opposing camps of distrust and enmity. . . .

Like other minority groups, Negroes will bear the major burden of their own progress. They will have to make their own way, as they are doing. But we must remember that other minorities, including my own, also made progress through increasing their political and economic power as well as by individual effort. Nor was that progress completely without violence, fear and hatred.

Moreover, earlier immigrants often began their climb by moving to the unsettled West, a door now closed; by finding unskilled labor, a door which is swiftly narrowing. Today to find a job requires increasingly complex skills denied to those without education. Nor did other minorities suffer under the special handicaps of the Negro heritage — centuries of slavery and a century of oppression, an intricate web of legal disabilities, and the crushing forces of racial feeling from whose poisons few whites have fully liberated themselves.

Thus, the changed circumstances of modern life and the peculiar nature of the Negro experience make large-scale Government action necessary if we are to crush the remaining barriers to equal opportunity. . . . We can never move too fast by giving men the liberty they were guaranteed a century ago. . . .

October 23, 1966
Berkeley campus
University of California

"I do not run for the Presidency merely to oppose any man, but to propose new policies. . . . to close the gaps between black and white, rich and poor, young and old, in this country and around the world."

Senators Robert and Edward Kennedy seek a few rare moments of relaxation and private conversation together.

If Congress can, and does, control the service of oleomargarine in every restaurant in the nation, surely it can insure our nonwhite citizens access to those restaurants.

If Congress can control the labeling of every bottle of aspirin in every drug store, surely it is not deprivating anyone's liberty to permit Negroes to shop and eat there. . . . Surely, it is no greater an infringement [on private rights] to compel nondiscrimination than it has been to compel discrimination.

There has been a good deal of talk decrying the Negro demonstrations. I say that any discussion of this problem which dwells solely on the demonstrations and not on the causes of these demonstrations is not going to solve anything.

. . . Repression on one side often produces violence on the other. The Haymarket riot of 1886, the violence of the Little Steel strike of 1938 and hundreds of similar incidents, large and small, are tragic cases in point.

But we learned from them and concentrated our attention upon the substantive evils that gave rise to the outbreaks. That is what the Interstate Public Accommodations Act of 1963 attempts to do, to concentrate upon the evils which have caused the recent demonstrations.

For most of the past hundred years, we have imposed the duties of citizenship on the Negro without allowing him to enjoy the benefits. We have demanded that he obey the same laws as white men, pay the same taxes, fight and die in the same wars. Yet, in nearly every part of the country, he remains the victim of humiliation and deprivation no white citizen would tolerate.

. . . We believe, therefore, that the Federal Government has no moral choice but to take the initiative [in civil rights]. How can we say to a Negro in Jackson, "When a war comes you will be an American citizen, but in the meantime, you're a citizen of Mississippi and we can't help you."

How, by any moral standard, can we tell our Negro citizens, "Our forefathers brought your forefathers here against their will, and we are going to make you pay for it."

Yet, isn't that just what the argument boils down to?

The United States is dominated by white people, politically and economically. The question is whether we, in this position of dominance, are going to have not the charity but the wisdom to stop penalizing our fellow citizens whose only fault or sin is that they were born.

July 1, 1963
Senate Commerce Committee
Hearing on Public Accommodations Bill

The effects of discrimination in public establishments are not limited to the embarrassment and frustration suffered by the individuals who are its most immediate victims. Our whole economy suffers when large retail stores or places of amusement whose goods have been obtained through interstate commerce, artificially restrict the market. . .

Business organizations in this country are increasingly mobile and interdependent.

. . . Artificial restrictions on their employees limit this type of mobility and its benefits to the national economy.

Further, if we add together only a minor portion of all the discriminatory acts throughout the country in any one year which deny food and lodging to Negroes, it is not difficult at all to see how, in the aggregate, interstate travel and interstate movement of goods in commerce may be substantially affected . . . commerce in these circumstances is discouraged, stifled, and restrained among the states as to provide an appropriate basis for Congressional action under the commerce clause. . . .

June 26, 1963
House Judiciary Committee
Hearing on civil rights
legislation

We've again betrayed our Indian people in not preparing them for the world. I'm distressed and shocked over our inattention to the Indian problem. We've broken our promises many times.

January 5, 1968
Visit to Western Indian School
Sherman Institute
Riverside, California

No white citizen would tolerate the humiliation and the deprivations...

"Prejudice still prevents many people. . . from attaining their full share of freedom. . . ."

The present National Origins quota system should be changed so that immigrants are admitted to this country on the basis of their qualifications and worth rather than on the basis of their place of birth or that of their ancestors.

That such conditions [social and economic oppressions] can be allowed to prevail among a people uniquely entitled to call themselves first Americans is nothing less than a national disgrace.

September 13, 1963
20th annual convention of the
National Congress of Indians
Bismarck, North Dakota

Prejudice still prevents many people of the Jewish faith from attaining their full share of the freedom, the equal opportunity, the untrammelled right to the pursuit of happiness that are so clearly promised in our Declaration of Independence and our Constitution.

. . . There are other, subtler but no less sinister forces of prejudice at work in America today — against Indians, Puerto Ricans, against Mexicans, against people of Japanese, Chinese and Philippine ancestry.

July 14, 1963
Slovak Catholic Sokol Convention
Youngstown, Ohio

The present National Origins quota system is a standing affront to millions of American citizens and to many countries. . . . It implies that regardless of individual qualifications, a man or woman born in Italy, or Greece, or Poland, or Portugal, or Czechoslovakia or the Ukraine is not as good as someone born in Ireland or England or Germany or Sweden. Everywhere else in our national life, we have eliminated discrimination based on one's place of birth. Yet this system is still the foundation of our immigration law.

July 22, 1964

It is my firm conviction that this National Origins system causes our nation great harm both at home and abroad, and that it should be eradicated from our law.

This National Origins system was conceived in a spirit of mistrust of certain racial groups in southern and eastern Europe and elsewhere. Its original stated purpose was bold discrimination — to preserve what was believed to be the racial and ethnic composition of our population in 1924.

This system is a blot on our relations with other countries. It violates our basic national philosophy because it judges individuals not on their worth, but solely on their place of birth — or even where their ancestors happened to be born. I know from my own experiences abroad how deeply this system hurts us. I have been asked how a country which professes that all men are equal could permit a system which treated immigrants so unequally. It is a difficult criticism to answer.

This system fails to fulfill our own needs at home. An unskilled laborer from a northern European country can come here without delay or difficulty. But . . . there are no visas now available for a Korean radiation expert, a Japanese microbiologist, a Greek chemist, a skilled teacher of the deaf from the Philippines — and many others like them. . . . The time has come for us to insist that the quota system be replaced by the merit system. . . .

Criticism of our National Origins quota system is difficult to answer...

"If we deny a man his place in the larger community then he may turn
inside to find his identity . . . rejecting those [who] have rejected him."

Robert Kennedy seemed able to identify closely
with the dispossessed of almost every society.

The National Origins quota system makes it easier for a man
to bring a maid to this country than to bring his mother; a system
which can so distort human values must be revised. . . .

. . . This system damages America in the eyes of the world. It
deprives us of able immigrants whose contributions we need. It
inflicts needless personal cruelty on large numbers of American
citizens and residents. And it doesn't work. Certainly, no plainer
or more compelling arguments could be made for changing this
system.

August 14, 1964
Letter to editor of *New York Times*

*Our efforts to banish all
prejudice must quicken...*

We must accelerate our efforts to banish religious prejudice, racial
discrimination and any intolerance which denies to any American
the rights guaranteed them by the Declaration of Independence and
the Constitution. That is what this [Cuban] crisis is all about. . . .
They [American forces] are there [in other countries] for the same
reason that the Maccabees stood their ground against Antiochus —
for human dignity and freedom. . . .

October 28, 1962
American Jewish Congress
New York, New York

59

V

The Inner City
and the Urban Environment

"The plight of the cities—the physical decay and human despair that pervades them—is the great internal problem of the American nation...."

Robert F. Kennedy realized early the crucial importance of cities in the future of America: "The cities are centers of culture, fashion, finance and industry, of sports and communications, for us all; and thus the center of the possibilities of American life. They are also the center of the problems of American life." He was also aware that of all our problems, the most immediate and pressing, the one that threatens to paralyze our capacity to act — "is the plight of the ghettos of our inner cities." Even without the problems of race, we would be faced with unemployment, inadequate housing and education.

Kennedy believed that our policies must be shaped "to make the inner cities places where men can raise families and live a decent life, and to give the men of the ghetto the opportunity to develop their own talents and realize their own potentialities." However, he stated that before this can be achieved, we "must understand past mistakes," such as a public housing policy which too often "tore down one slum and built another." Other basic errors have been made in "total reliance on government" and the failure to see that employment is "the key" to dissolving the ghetto. Such mistakes can be rectified by bringing "government back to the people of the neighborhood" and creating at this level Community Development Corporations which would enlist the help of private enterprise, in addition to government, to "ensure that what is done to create jobs and build homes builds the community as well."

Another major problem that affects entire metropolitan areas to which Kennedy gave considerable attention was the increasing pollution of water and the air we breathe. Here, too, a significant effort had to be made because "we cannot wait for technology to make clean air entirely painless. . . . Technological progress may reduce costs later . . . but we all pay . . . now."

Opposite page: "Without even counting the cost to human life and health — for these are literally beyond price — it is clear that air pollution costs the people of New York at least $1 billion a year. . . ."

Private industry, working through Community Development Corporations, could provide jobs within the ghetto.

The genius of America is its ability to meet all challenges...

The plight of the cities — the physical decay and human despair that pervades them — is the great internal problem of the American nation, a challenge which must be met. The peculiar genius of America has been its ability, in the face of such challenges, to summon all our resources of mind and body, to focus these resources and our attention and effort, in whatever amount is necessary, to solve the deepest and most resistant problems. That is the commitment and the spirit required in our cities today.

January 20, 1967
Buffalo Model City Conference
Buffalo, New York

The New York World's Fair exemplifies the scientific advances of the twentieth century and it offers suggestions about the America of the twenty-first century. But less than an hour away in Harlem, people live in squalor and despair more closely resembling the nineteenth century.

June 7, 1964
Marquette University
Milwaukee, Wisconsin

We have seen the unemployed as a problem and provided welfare; but men need work. We have seen physical misery as a problem and built housing; but men need communities in which to live. And we have seen the residents of these ghettos as afflicted with problems of person and family and prescribed more psychiatrists and social workers and guidance counselors; but men need these helpers far less than they need the chance to contribute to themselves, their families, and their community — to stand with pride in themselves and with respect among their fellows.

Without work — and community — and true opportunity to stand as men and citizens, the basic right, the right to be human, cannot be fulfilled.

May 11, 1966
New York Pre-White House Conference
on Civil Rights

We have the ideas, the programs and the men to win the battle against poverty, idleness and despair...

Of all our failures in dealing with the problems of the poor, the greatest is the failure to provide jobs. Here is an aspect of our cities' problems almost untouched by Federal action. No government program now operating gives any substantial promise of meeting the problem of unemployment in the inner city, and thus of any way to avoid the inefficient, wastefully expensive, degrading and self-defeating system of welfare.

From *To Seek a Newer World*
by Robert F. Kennedy

We must look for action [to improve economic conditions and end riots] in two stages. The first is an immediate impact project designed to put man to work and restore hope to the young and to give the unemployed resident of the city slum some sense of dignity and promise.

We should begin immediate programs of needed public tasks and jobs — providing jobs to build schools and roads, to restore parks and erect clinics, and to staff the schools and clinics and neighborhood centers when they are built.

Our communities need these jobs done and the men of the ghetto need jobs. By matching the two we can return hope while meeting the most urgent needs of the nation. . . .

We must enlist not merely the Federal Government, as we have done through the war on poverty and other programs, but local authority and private enterprise, the skill and resources of the entire nation.

We must turn the power and resources of our private enterprise system to the underdeveloped nation within our midst. This should be done by bringing into the ghettos themselves productive and profitable private industry, creating dignified jobs, not welfare handouts, for the men and youth who now languish in idleness. . . .

Beyond this, we need an all-encompassing program to strike at the sources of urban poverty. We have ideas, we have programs. And we have men willing to carry forward the battle against poverty and hopelessness.

What we need now is the leadership at every level, committed to ending the conditions which spur men to revolt in the streets of our cities.

Violence is wrong, but it is also a reminder. It is a reminder that millions of American citizens have been shut out from the blessing of American freedom. It is a reminder of our common failure to ensure opportunity to the black man and the American Indian, to the Mexican-American and the Puerto Rican, to all of the oppressed in our midst. It is a reminder that the American promise is still unfulfilled.

August 4, 1967
Democratic legislative dinner
San Francisco, California

We cannot leave our children a legacy of chaos.

We once thought public housing was the answer. But as one woman in the Pruitt-Igoe project in St. Louis said, "They were trying to better poor people. They tore down one slum and built another." The projects were built without asking what would become of the people who would live in them — where or even whether they would work, where their children would go to school, what they would do when they were sick, even how they would travel downtown — in short, without asking how to solve the problems that caused them to need assistance in the first place. Too many of the projects, as a result, became places of despair and danger for their residents: plagued by high vacancy rates, stealing, mugging, and public drinking.

From *To Seek a Newer World*
by Robert F. Kennedy

Let us make room at the table of fulfillment for our ghetto brothers...

We have created a welfare system which aids only a fourth of those who are poor, which forces men to leave their families so that public assistance can be obtained, which has created a dependence on their fellow citizens that is degrading and distasteful to giver and receiver alike. . . .

We have built vast, impersonal, high-rise public housing projects — ghettos within ghettos — isolated from the outside world and devoid of any sense of humanity. . . .

We have cleaned areas of slums in the name of urban renewal, with little sense of what would become of those whose homes we leveled. . . .

May 8, 1967
Symposium: "The Child & The City," sponsored
by Day Care Council of New York
New York, New York

If there were no "man-in-the-house" rule, if welfare were not cut off dollar for dollar as earnings of an A.D.C. mother increase, if welfare were available to supplement the earnings of a working father who does not earn subsistence pay. . . . If, in short, welfare were a system based on need instead of artificial categories, many of those 3.5 million children would have working fathers living at home.

June 9, 1967
Open forum on welfare sponsored by Community
Council of Greater New York
New York, New York

Reliance on government is dependence, and what the people of our ghettos need is not greater dependence but full independence; not the charity and favor of their fellow citizens but equal claims of right and equal power to enforce those claims. . . .

What is new, what must be different in the effort ahead is the combination of job creation, education and physical reconstruction on a scale large enough to meet the needs of all our people. . . .

In these last five years, we have asked the people of our urban ghettos to the breakfast of hope, but the supper of fulfillment we eat without them. Breakfast has long ago been eaten, and hunger walks the streets. It is time to make room at the table.

May 18, 1966
Meeting of NAACP
Legal Defense and Educational
Fund, Inc.

"The loss of the sense of community is not just a problem of the ghetto; it affects all of us. . . . In far too many places . . . the home is a place to sleep and eat and watch television; but where it is located is not a community."

In some programs, a chance to bring the government back to the people...

Bedford-Stuyvesant is more than an experiment in economic and social development. It is an experiment in politics, an experiment in self-government. Indeed, it is above all a chance to bring government back to the people of the neighborhood. For the loss of the sense of community is not just a problem of the ghetto; it affects all of us. Housing developments spring up, but there is no real place for people to walk, for women and their children to meet, for common activities. The place of work is far away through blackened tunnels or over congested highways. The doctor and lawyer and government official are often somewhere else and hardly known. In far too many places — in pleasant suburbs as well as city streets — the home is a place to sleep and eat and watch television; but where it is located is not a community. We live in too many places and so we live nowhere. Long ago De Tocqueville foresaw the fate of people without community: "Each of them living apart is a stranger to the fate of all the rest — his children and his private friends constitute to him the whole of mankind; as for the rest of his fellow citizens, he is close to them, but he seeks them not; he touches them but he feels them not . . . he may be said at any rate to have lost his country."

Lewis Mumford observed recently that "democracy, in any active sense, begins and ends in communities small enough for their members to meet face to face." One may argue about the ideal size, but certainly there are strong arguments to support the decentralization of some municipal functions and some aspects of government into smaller units, no matter what the race or economic status of the governed, no matter whether they live in center city or suburb.

The plight of our cities was a concern of both Senator Kennedy and Mayor John Lindsay of New York City.

From *To Seek a Newer World*
by Robert F. Kennedy

The promise of America — opportunity for all — will be fulfilled when we turn our full attention and all our resources to the underdeveloped nation within our midst.

Many people are born into a life of squalor and despair from which escape is nearly impossible.

Our greatest failure in dealing with the problem of poverty has been the failure to provide jobs. Without the dignity of work, man cannot have a sense of pride in himself.

These children will have a chance — there is still tir. if we will declare their environment a national eme.

Many children would have working fathers who lived at home if welfare had no "man-in-the-house" rule.

"We have built . . . ghettos within ghettos — isolated from the outside world and devoid of humanity."

Hope can be restored to our youth if we are willing to act upon the ills of our society.

"Solutions of the 1930's are not the solutions of today . . . we are a new generation. . . ."

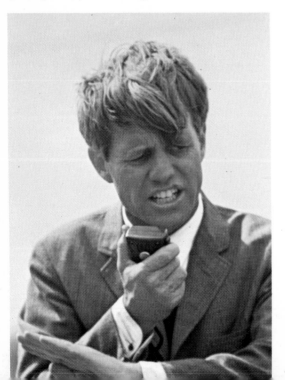

To many among us, a promise remains unfulfilled...

Direct relationship between the Federal Government and the cities has worked well in programs like urban renewal. Obviously, effective action in both of these fields depends upon cooperation among the Federal, state and local governments. But some means should be possible for communities to take advantage of Federal programs without unreasonable vetoes being superimposed by the states.

[In response to the question: "Do you favor cities dealing directly with the Federal Government on programs like . . . slum clearance, etc., or do you believe all dealings should be through the state?"]

October 11, 1964

. . . The heart not only of the private enterprise program, but of nearly all programs aimed at alleviating slum conditions should be the creation of Community Development Corporations. Such corporations might be financed by an initial contribution of capital from the Federal Government; but for their ongoing activities, they would need and receive no significantly greater subsidy than is ordinarily available to nonprofit corporations under present law.

The community corporations would ensure that what is done to create jobs and build homes builds the community as well, and builds new and continuing opportunities for its residents. They would ensure that what is done involves not just the physical development of the community, but the development of its educational system, its health services — in short, all the services its residents need. They would be the source of technical assistance to local businessmen. And they would be the main channel through which outside aid — government or private — enters the community. They would have the opportunity to make every government program, and many private efforts, more effective than ever before.

From *To Seek a Newer World*
by Robert F. Kennedy

Above: The impersonality of urban dwellings is characterized in this aerial view of apartments in south San Francisco.

Community Development Corporations could serve all residents' needs...

Right: Adequate assistance should be provided in a dignified manner for those who are no longer able to work.

. . . We should not — we cannot — wait for technology to make clean air entirely painless, to be achieved without effort, like a genie waving a magic wand. We will never get anywhere unless we begin now to apply what we do know. Technological progress may reduce costs later; that will be all to the good. But we all pay for air pollution now, every day. Without even counting the cost to human life and health — for these are literally beyond price — it is clear that air pollution costs the people of New York at least $1 billion a year — $70 for every man, woman, and child in the metropolitan area. That cost we pay every day; surely we can invest one-tenth of that amount to save ourselves the other nine-tenths.

We should, I believe, beware of the pitfalls described by Twain:

> Imagine a man who sets out on a voyage equipped with a pair of spectacles that magnify things to an extraordinary degree. A hair on his hand, a spot on the tablecloth, the shifting of a coat, all will attract his attention; at this rate, he will not go far, he will spend his day taking six steps and will never get out of his room.

We have to get out of the room.

> January 4, 1967
> New York-New Jersey Metropolitan Area
> Air Pollution Control Conference

We should begin to apply now what we know in the pollution control area...

Above: Rubbish dumps and automobile graveyards such as this one often mar the rural scenery near small towns.
Opposite page: Air pollution and its consequent effect on health and safety is one of the most pressing of urban problems.

State and local governments can lead in resource management...

Senator Kennedy recognized that "we cannot wait for technology" to solve problems of air and water pollution.

On a trip to Latin America last year, I saw people in Recife, in the poorest part of Brazil, who ate crabs which lived off the garbage that the people themselves threw in the shallow water near their shabby rooms. And whenever I tell this story to Americans, the reaction is: How sad, how terrible, that such poverty, such under-development, should exist in the world!

But we New Yorkers are in a poor position from which to extend pity. For every year the average New Yorker — old and young, rich and poor, athlete or infirm recluse — breathes in 750 pounds of his own wastes. The fuel which generates our electricity, the gasoline which runs our cars and taxicabs and buses, the four pounds of trash and garbage which each of us gives the city each day, and even the garbage we drop into our apartment-house incinerators — all these are discharged into the air we breathe. And because there are so many of us crowding into this tiny fraction of the United States, a great pall of filthy air blankets the entire metropolitan area — and we all must breathe the same air into which we carelessly spill our refuse.

January 4, 1967
New York-New Jersey Metropolitan Area
Air Pollution Control Conference

The Federal Power Commission, perhaps in cooperation with the Atomic Energy Commission and the Department of Commerce, should review our uses of fuels, atomic, fossil and chemical, as they relate to pollution. Such a review could provide useful standards for fuel combustion in metropolitan areas and provide a guideline for utilization of fuels.

. . . The continuing contamination of New York City's air threatens both the health and safety of its many residents.

Although experts agree that air pollution is rarely responsible for the loss of life by itself, when combined with respiratory or circulatory disease it can take a toll of human life. It particularly affects our older citizens with respiratory problems; as the number of older citizens increases the danger of air pollution increases proportionately.

June 26, 1965

[The polluted Hudson River] is such a wasted asset. This could be a beach where people could swim and play. We have such tremendous natural resources, it's a crime against the present generation and against our children and our children's children to waste it like this. . . . the initiative has to be taken by the state and local governments.

May 2, 1965
Inspection of Hudson River
New York, New York

Right: Our children's lives may one day depend on how we use natural resources now.

Below: Through visionary planning and conservation, our rivers and lakes can once again become safe recreational areas, but we must begin immediately.

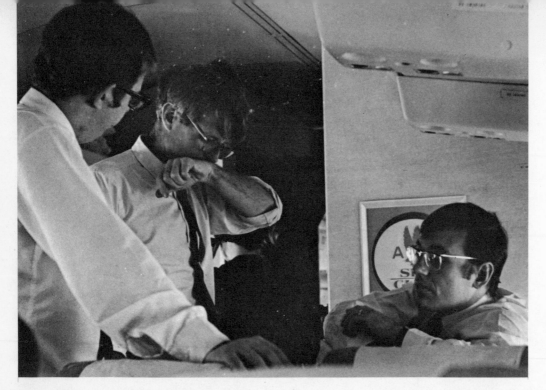

Above: "What we need is leadership at every level. . . ."

Below: Our urban life has created a situation in which men are strangers to one another because they are without community.

Human beings need a purpose, a job to do, a sense of self-worth...

There is still time, if we treat our urban dilemma as the national emergency it so clearly is. There is still time, if our response in concern and resources proves we are willing to rescue our cities from chaos. The chance is there.

April 11, 1968
Lansing, Michigan

We must return local control to the people themselves. In the last analysis, it should be in the cities and towns and villages where the decisions are made, not in Washington.

Solutions of the 1930's are not the solutions of today. The solutions of the New Frontier are not necessarily applicable now. We are a new generation with new problems. I run for President because I believe in the ideas of this generation, and I believe I can do better.

We need a new kind of program which places money directly into communities, instead of flowing through an inefficient, over-structured, often tyrannical bureaucracy which is too often immobilized by sheer size to act swiftly and directly.

March 27, 1968
Salt Lake City, Utah

The answer to the welfare crisis is work, jobs, self-sufficiency and family integrity; not a massive new extension of welfare; not a great new outpouring of guidance counselors to give the poor more advice. . . .

Human beings need a purpose. We can achieve that purpose if we develop a system where there are jobs at decent pay for all who are able to work; and adequate assistance provided in a dignified way for those who are unable to work.

May 18, 1968
Washington, D. C.

By creating programs for needed public works such as highway construction (above) and the erection of schools and hospitals (below) we can provide jobs for the unemployed.

VI
The America to Come

"We are a nation which has reached the height of its power and influence at a time when the old order of things is crumbling and the new world is painfully struggling to take shape. It is a moment as fully charged with opportunity as that granted to Columbus or the heroes of the Italian Renaissance."

Robert F. Kennedy was not given to illusions and yet through everything—wars of questionable purpose, assassinations, crime, injustice and riots—he never lost faith in his country. While criticizing and warning of many of the same things as the gloomy prophets and doom-sayers, he always maintained an indomitable belief in the better America that was to come. It was probably partly due to his own natural energy and ebullience, as well as his pragmatic turn of mind, his competitive spirit and his belief in the power of the individual human will. It also probably had something to do with the legacy of fortitude so evident in his tragedy-scarred family. But specifically it seems to have been rooted in his refusal to see in difficulties, no matter how enormous, anything other than challenge and opportunity. To Robert Kennedy, for a nation (or statesman) to be at the height of its (or his) power as an old order crumbled and a new one took shape, was a moment charged with possibility, a chance for great achievement. In a world of change and turmoil, we must "master change." He believed, with Emerson, that "God gives to each of us the choice between truth and repose. Take which you please. You cannot have both."

Opposite page: Silent crowds file slowly into St. Patrick's Cathedral in New York City in a final tribute to the assassinated Senator Robert Kennedy.

We are a nation which has reached the height of its power and influence at a time when the old order of things is crumbling and the new world is painfully struggling to take shape. It is a moment as fully charged with opportunity as that granted to Columbus or the heroes of the Italian Renaissance. It offers to this nation the chance for great achievement — or perhaps the greatest and most destructive of failures. It is a voyage more hazardous and uncertain than that which we celebrate today. For we seek to cross the dark and storm-scarred seas of human passion and unreason, ignorance and anger. These were as uncharted in Columbus' time as they are today. Yet we have been thrust upon them by our mastery of the continent he discovered and the knowledge his age began. The way is uncertain, and the trip is charged with hazard. Yet perhaps we can say, in the words of Garibaldi to his followers: "I do not promise you ease. I do not promise you comfort. But I do promise you these: hardship, weariness, and suffering. And with them, I promise you victory."

October 11, 1966
Columbus Day Dinner
New York, New York

This is not the easiest time in the life of the United States because the American people bear unusual and heavy burdens. It is easier for some, perhaps, to find solace and comfort and satisfaction in old slogans, old theories and easy answers rather than to examine the facts, consider the future and face up to our responsibilities with the full realization that there are no easy answers.

June 12, 1962
Manhattan College
New York, New York

We have it within our power to give to millions of . . . young people a greater chance at a decent life — to now have a major effect on the course of their next thirty or forty years. Millions are without schools — and we can help to build schoolrooms; millions more are without textbooks, or teachers — and we can help to provide textbooks and train teachers; others cannot eat — and we have food.

Clean water, better housing, education and training, a job to look forward to — these things we can help to provide.

And we must.

Opportunities lost to these young people now, as we have found to our sorrow here at home, will be far harder to make up later. But a relatively modest investment can make a difference, in fifty or one hundred years, to as much as half the world's people — including our own.

For our legacy — to our children, to the next generation of political leaders in the United States — will be far more than what we leave within our boundaries. Its most important element will be the role and standing of the United States in the world — whether, in short, people will look to this country with hope or with hate, emulation or envy.

July 21, 1966
U. S. Senate

We must realize that in these times there are no easy answers to problems...

"*It is not enough to understand, or to see clearly. The future will be shaped in the arena of human activity by those willing to commit their minds and bodies. . . .*"

Every question requires new thinking and the willingness to dare...

Our gross national product now soars above $800 billion a year. But that counts air pollution and cigarette advertising and ambulances to clear highways of carnage. It counts the special locks for our doors and jails for the people who break them. It counts the destruction of our redwoods and the loss of natural wonder to chaotic sprawl.

It counts napalm and nuclear warheads and armored cars for the police to fight riots in our cities. It counts Whitman's rifle and Speck's knife and television programs which glorify violence to sell toys to our children.

March 10, 1968
Farm workers' rally
Delano, California

We can slow down the race to the moon, if it means the salvation of our nation here on earth. We can postpone work on the supersonic transport, if it means that we can safely sit in our cities.

April 11, 1968
Kalamazoo, Michigan

The crisis of our cities, the tension of our races, the complexities of a society at once so rich and so deprived — all these call urgently for the best effort of all Americans all across this country.

We must reach across the false barriers that divide us from brothers and from countrymen to seek and find peace abroad, reconciliation at home and the participation in the life of our country. That is the deepest desire of the American people and the truest expression of our national goals.

April 1, 1968
News Conference
Overseas Press Club
New York, New York

Below and right: The violence within our country may be ended if the nation will look beyond the demonstrations and riots to the reasons for these forms of protest.

There is no question which does not require . . . new thinking — the same willingness to dare.

We have grown accustomed to fighting for school desegregation in the South; but are we ready to institute the reforms necessary for true desegregation in the North?

We have grown accustomed to building public housing in the ghetto and writing fair-housing laws for our statute books; but will we build housing that Negroes can afford outside the slums and center cities?

We have committed our surplus food to feed the starving abroad, and we have offered to help in curbing population growth; but will we act on the scale necessary to prevent the mass starvation which our present level of effort cannot forestall?

We ourselves must change to master change. We must rethink all our old ideas and beliefs before they capture and destroy us. And, for those answers, America must look to its young people, the children of this time of change. And we look especially to that privileged minority of educated men who are the students of America.

And answers founded on clear and dispassionate thought must be matched to action, rooted to conviction and a passionate desire to reshape the world. It is not enough to understand, or, to see clearly. The future will be shaped in the arena of human activity by those willing to commit their minds and bodies to the past. Ralph Waldo Emerson said, "God gives to each of us the choice between truth and repose. Take which you please. You cannot have both."

September 17, 1966
Worthington, Minnesota

To "muddle through a crisis" was once a democratic people's boast. That self-indulgent day is gone. There is no time now for confusion and no place for perplexities.

November 18, 1961
School of Law
Fordham University
New York, New York

[About Goldwater's campaign for Presidency:]

Fixed answers are no answers at all in a changing world. They are rather a response of frustration to the tides of change, which no man can predict, shape, or repeal.

The future does not belong to such men of rigid certitude.

June 26, 1964
Free University of Berlin
Berlin, Germany

There is a need for individual participation [in the task of human betterment]. All of us have to participate. All of us are needed. The question is whether to be a critic or a participant. The question is whether to bring a candle to the barricade or to curse the darkness.

June 27, 1964
Heidelburg University
West Germany

As Attorney General, Robert Kennedy became one of President John F. Kennedy's principal advisors.

Reach out over the barriers that divide us, brother from brother, and find peace...

Ethel Kennedy listens intently as her husband explains his decision to run for the office of President.

A fast-paced game of football was a traditional Kennedy way of relaxing with the family.

If we now begin to rebuild all the inadequate housing, to erect all the new schools, to repair our crumbling hospitals, to provide parks and playgrounds, renovate our beaches, refurbish our subways — in this infinite inventory there will be work enough for all our people ... thousands could discover their potential in this rebuilding effort.

We can and must do what needs doing at home; the richest nation in the history of the world can afford to share its riches with all its citizens.

May 11, 1966
New York Pre-White House
Conference on Civil Rights

Yes, we have our problems in Alabama, but to be blunt, we are not shooting old women and young children in the back as the communists are doing in Berlin. As the newspapers and people of the world freely discuss the errors of a small minority in this country and hold the entire United States responsible, the communist officials themselves build a wall in Berlin to keep truth and freedom out — and tyranny in. Those who attempt to flee the Worker's Paradise receive a bullet — not a passport.

Can anybody equate the disturbance in Alabama last spring with the death by starvation of hundreds and hundreds of thousands of Chinese peasants under a farm-commune system which has failed?

Consider how many thousands of words have been printed around the world about Birmingham and Montgomery compared to what has been said about this systematic extinction of large numbers of Chinese by their fellow countrymen. How much more has been written about Little Rock than Tibet or even Hungary!

This is a free society. Our faults are discussed. Our mistakes make a rich grist for the communist propaganda machine. This we accept. However, let us all remember also that their failures are seldom even mentioned, their mistakes never fully known, and the terror of their system discussed only when it becomes a political expedient. Five years after Khrushchev dies — who will be moving his body?

December 3, 1961
National Conference of
Christians and Jews dinner
Cleveland, Ohio

The adventure of change may be a tragic adventure for many — a sad uprooting of cherished customs and institutions. Yet change is the one constant of history. It has certainly been the dominating fact in the development of my own country. From the first moment of independence, the United States has been dedicated to innovation as a way of government and a way of life. Not a decade has gone by in our nation's history in which we did not undergo new experiences and seek new challenges. We were born in a revolution against colonialism, and we have been dedicated ever since to a revolution for freedom and progress.

We have been dedicated since colonial times to a revolution for freedom and progress...

Above all other things, this nation is dedicated to the dignity of individuals...

My country has not been alone in pursuing these aims, and, like all countries, the United States has made its share of mistakes. But at its best and its most characteristic, the United States has been, above all, a progressive nation — a nation dedicated to the enlargement of opportunity for those President Andrew Jackson described as the humble members of society — the farmers, mechanics, and laborers.

The United States is a nation dedicated to the emancipation of women, to the education of children, and, above all, to the dignity of the individual. This commitment to "life, liberty and the pursuit of happiness" has inspired the essential motive of our national life — the unceasing search for new frontiers, not only frontiers of geography, but also frontiers of science and technology and social and political invention and human freedom. These are the new frontiers which must be challenged and conquered by our generation — yours and mine. We must meet these problems and still maintain our dedication to democracy and freedom. To do so we must be imaginative and creative — not blindly wedded to the past. How to accomplish this task is the struggle for the people of every country and for the governments of all nations. We in the United States are willing to meet these challenges as I know you are.

We in my country are by disposition and inheritance a people mistrustful of absolute doctrines and ideologies, persuaded that reason and experiment are the means by which free people fulfill their purposes. Yet we live in a century obsessed with ideology — a century that has been filled with leaders persuaded that they were the possessors of absolute truth, and that all must do as they say — or perish.

February 6, 1962
Nihon University
Tokyo, Japan

I am announcing today my candidacy for the Presidency of the United States.

I do not run for the Presidency merely to oppose any man, but to propose new policies. I run because I am convinced that this country is on a perilous course and because I have such strong feelings about what must be done, and I feel that I'm obliged to do all that I can.

I run to seek new policies — policies to end the bloodshed in Vietnam and in our cities, policies to close the gap that now exists between black and white, between rich and poor, between young and old in this country and around the rest of the world.

I run for the Presidency because I want the Democratic Party and the United States of America to stand for hope instead of despair, for reconciliation of men instead of the growing risk of world war.

I run because it is now unmistakably clear that we can change these disastrous, divisive policies only by changing the men who are now making them. For the reality of recent events in Vietnam has been glossed over with illusions.

March 16, 1968
News Conference when he announced
candidacy for the Presidency
Washington, D. C.

Opposite page: "It is a willingness to die that makes it possible to live."

Our efforts must be to tran-scend violence with love...

Robert Kennedy kneels by the grave of his assassi-nated brother, the late President John F. Kennedy.

The Kennedys visit with Mrs. King after the assassination of Dr. Martin Luther King, Jr.

Above: It is important that we continue our striving for excellence.

It is up to those of us who are here to carry on the dream...

Left: "I dream things that never were and say, why not."

"I believe this nation has the chance for great achievement."

It is within our power to provide a decent life for all...

I'd like to harness all the energy and effort and incentive and imagination that was attracted to Government by President Kennedy. I don't want any of that to die. It is important that this striving for excellence should continue, that there be an end to mediocrity. The torch really has passed to a new generation. People are still looking for all that idealism. It permeated young people all over the globe. And I became sort of a symbol, not just as an individual.

July 6, 1964
Newsweek interview

We do not propose to let the possibilities of that greatness [for humanity] be overwhelmed by those who would lock us all into the narrow tunnels of a dark and rigid system. We will defend our faith [in democracy] by affirmation, by argument, if necessary — and heaven forbid that it should become necessary — by arms. It is a willingness to die that makes it possible to live.

February 5, 1962
Visit to working-class bar
Tokyo, Japan

90

We wonder if we still hold a decent respect for the opinions of mankind, and whether that opinion maintains a decent respect for us — or whether, like Athens of old, we will forfeit sympathy and support alike, and ultimately our very security, in a single-minded pursuit of our own goals and objectives.

[Democrats this year before the American people] must account to them in honesty and candor: proud enough of our successes to admit our past shortcomings; open enough about our failures so that we can put them right in the future.

March 9, 1968
Des Moines, Iowa

I don't think you can go to the American people and say everything is satisfactory in America. It is not satisfactory to say that Americans own 70 million television sets when what you see on those sets is rioting, violence and disorder. . . .

For those who have affluence it is easy to say this is the politics of happiness, but if you see children starving in the Delta of Mississippi and the despair on the Indian reservations, then you know that everything in America is not satisfactory.

May 15, 1968
Kennedy Square
Detroit, Michigan

I think we can end the divisions in the United States. What I think is quite clear is that we can work together in the last analysis.

And that is what has been going on within the United States over a period of the last three years — the division, the violence, the disenchantment with our society, the division, whether it's between black and whites, between the poor and the more affluent, between age groups, or in the war on Vietnam — that we can start to work together.

We are a great country, an unselfish country and a compassionate country. And I intend to make that my basis for running.

We want to deal with our own problems in our own country and we want peace in Vietnam.

So my thanks to all of you and it's on to Chicago and let's win there.

June 4, 1968
Victory speech after winning
California Primary
Los Angeles, California

Let us be open about our failures so that we may put them right in the future...

Robert Kennedy once remarked that the most important decision he had ever made was "marrying Ethel."

Epilogue:
The Personal Vision

"Sorrow is a form of self-pity. . . . and we have to go on."

How does one come to know the private side of a public man one has never known personally? The answer is that, despite the flood of mass-media articles and interviews and many sincere efforts, one never really can know them. Our curiosity is left with little more than a series of images, often preconceived and manipulated for a variety of unrevealed purposes. This was especially true of Robert F. Kennedy. Images were produced to fit every side of his complex personality, as well as some that were pure fabrication. He was an apparent paradox, always energetic and usually outgoing, yet given to periods of solitary intro-spection. He was a rare mixture of bluntness and gentleness, ambition and compassion.

Perhaps there is no better way for those not privileged to have known him than to read a few of his thoughts on character and the human condition. If something of an enigma about him remains, one should remember that he once said: "The end of true learning is not to establish certainties but to achieve humility in the face of the unknowable."

Opposite page: An honor guard flanking the flag-draped casket of Senator Robert F. Kennedy included David Brinkley (left foreground) and Attorney General Ramsey Clark (left background).

*All Americans will have
to be leaders in the
difficult years ahead...*

I decided at quite a young age that I would dedicate myself to work for the Government. . . . in my estimation I think that I have had invaluable experience.

January 13, 1961
Investigation of Robert F. Kennedy
for Attorney General

When I came back here and tried to get people to fill the top jobs and found out how difficult it was, I felt that I had a duty to do my part.
. . . I realized then what an advantage it would be to him [John F. Kennedy] to have someone he could talk to.
[To a friend after accepting post of Attorney General.]

December 16, 1960

[About the 1972 Presidential campaign:]

I'm not going to direct my life to where I'll be in 1972. Six years is so far away; tomorrow is far away. I don't even know if I'll be alive in six years.

If a man gears every aspect of his life to a goal like winning the Presidency in a certain year and his timetable does not work out, his life becomes one of great frustration.

October 18, 1966

I believe that any who seek high office this year must go before all Americans, not just those who agree with them but also those who disagree; recognizing that it is not just our supporters, not just those who vote for us, but all Americans, who must lead in the difficult years ahead. And that is why I have come, at the outset of my campaign, not to New York or Chicago or Boston, but here to Alabama.

March 21, 1968
Tuscaloosa, Alabama

*Robert and Ethel Kennedy pose with their family of ten
near Hickory Hill, their home in McLean, Virginia.*

Joseph and Rose Kennedy relax with eight of their children. Young Robert is in front of John at left.

"Our finest convictions," said Ortega y Gasset, "are apt to be the most suspect. They mark our limitations and our bounds. Life is a petty thing unless it is moved by the indomitable urge to extend its boundaries."

One of our own great scientists, Robert Oppenheimer, put the same thought a different way when he was asked to define exactly what it was that scientists of his caliber did all day. They sit around, he said, explaining to each other the things they do not know.

I believe that wise men through the ages have always done just that — for surely the end of true learning is not to establish certainties but to achieve humility in the face of the unknowable.

September 23, 1963
New York, New York

. . . Ours is a time when many things are just too big to be grasped. It is a century which has heaped up enough explosive power to blow up the world. It is a century which has probed into the floor of the sea, which has flung men far into outer space, which now threatens to invade the moon.

When things are done on too vast a scale, the human imagination bogs down. It can no longer visualize such fantastic things and thus looses its grip on their essential reality. Killing one man is murder; killing millions is a statistic. The disclosures of the Eichmann trial remind us all how quickly the world has forgotten the massive horrors which one set of human beings perpetrated against another a short twenty years ago.

Our problems, having grown to the size of the world, if not the solar system, no longer seem our own. Each day we are required to respond to a new crisis created by people whose names we cannot pronounce, in lands of which we have never heard. After a time the capacity to respond begins to flag, and we turn not cheerfully, but almost in despair, to the sports pages and the comics.

And yet I would say to you that the stake is just as personal today as it was a century ago, the obligation just as personal, the capacity to affect the course of history just as great. What we require is not the self-indulgence of resignation from the world but the hard effort to work out new ways of fulfilling our personal concern and our personal responsibility.

June 21, 1961
Joint Defense Appeal of the American
Jewish Committee and the Anti-
Defamation League of the B'nai B'rith
Chicago, Illinois

We require new ways of fulfilling our individual concern and duties...

Through man's memory, the revelations of the past enter the structure of civilization to which each generation adds...

Senator Edward Kennedy escorts his sister-in-law Ethel to her pew during the funeral services for her husband.

Florence is an enemy to pride because it recounts one of the most powerful and constant lessons of history. The wars and conquests, the brilliantly complex politics and intrigue, the imperative concerns of state, have been covered by the same years which now cloak the colonial empire of Athens and the triumphs of Rome. They did leave an imprint. But it is the ideas and paintings, statues, philosophy and knowledge which endure most vividly, shaping and enriching our own lives. They instruct the future that the mastery of transient events, our accomplishments and victories, will ultimately matter less than what we contribute to the liberation of the human spirit.

Nor are the broken manuscripts and works of art simply the creations of our civilization. They are its source and substance. Many forms of life come together in carefully designed societies. Man alone has built civilizations, not just because he is intelligent or skillful, but because he can remember. Through that memory the ideas and revelations of the past enter the structure to which each generation adds. What has been damaged or destroyed in Florence is part of the fragile fabric of collective memory which binds our conflicting aims and actions into civilization.

Even this does not completely tell us why, in a world filled with destruction and tragedy, the flood of Florence should compel the concern of men and women in so many countries. In an age which has seen entire cities shattered in a moment and millions murdered by cold insanity, why does the sight of a stained painting or a broken door panel call forth sorrow and the pain of loss? It is not simply that the art and records are beautiful and priceless and irreplaceable. It is, rather, that they help redeem us from the terrible judgment of history on the wisdom and love of men. Man has built bombs, but he has also painted the crucifixion. He has expended rage in slaughter, but he has also labored to carve panels for a church or illuminate a manuscript.

January 6, 1967
Concert for Italian Flood Relief
Carnegie Hall
New York, New York

Robert Kennedy, Jr., walks the grounds of Hickory Hill with a friend of the family shortly after the death of his father.

What has violence ever accomplished? What has it ever created? No martyr's cause has ever been stilled by his assassin's bullet. No wrongs have ever been righted by riots and civil disorders. A sniper is only a coward, not a hero; and an uncontrolled, uncontrollable mob is only the voice of madness, not the voice of the people.

April 5, 1968
Cleveland City Club
Cleveland, Ohio

No assassin's bullet can still the cause for which a man has lived...

When I think of all the things that have happened since that snowy inauguration day in January [John F. Kennedy's inauguration], I like to think our role has been the one that is suggested in an old Greek saying: "To tame the savageness of man, make gentle the life of the world."

September 3, 1964

[Statement to a street corner rally of Negroes shortly after the death of Martin Luther King:]

"Even in our sleep, pain which cannot forget falls drop by drop upon the heart until in our own despair, against our will, comes wisdom through the awful grace of God." — Aeschylus

April 4, 1968
Indianapolis, Indiana

[About John F. Kennedy's death:]

Sorrow is a form of self-pity . . . and we have to go on.

97